# EVIDENCE-BASED TREATMENT PLANNING FOR BIPOLAR DISORDER

# EVIDENCE-BASED TREATMENT PLANNING FOR BIPOLAR DISORDER

## DVD FACILITATOR'S GUIDE

TIMOTHY J. BRUCE
AND
ARTHUR E. JONGSMA, JR.

John Wiley & Sons, Inc.

This book is printed on acid-free paper. ∞

Copyright © 2012 by Arthur E. Jongsma, Jr. and Timothy J. Bruce. All rights reserved.

Published by John Wiley & Sons, Inc., Hoboken, New Jersey.
Published simultaneously in Canada.

No part of this publication may be reproduced, stored in a retrieval system, or transmitted in any form or by any means, electronic, mechanical, photocopying, recording, scanning, or otherwise, except as permitted under Section 107 or 108 of the 1976 United States Copyright Act, without either the prior written permission of the Publisher, or authorization through payment of the appropriate per-copy fee to the Copyright Clearance Center, Inc., 222 Rosewood Drive, Danvers, MA 01923, (978) 750-8400, fax (978) 646-8600, or on the web at www.copyright.com. Requests to the Publisher for permission should be addressed to the Permissions Department, John Wiley & Sons, Inc., 111 River Street, Hoboken, NJ 07030, (201) 748-6011, fax (201) 748-6008.

Limit of Liability/Disclaimer of Warranty: While the publisher and author have used their best efforts in preparing this book, they make no representations or warranties with respect to the accuracy or completeness of the contents of this book and specifically disclaim any implied warranties of merchantability or fitness for a particular purpose. No warranty may be created or extended by sales representatives or written sales materials. The advice and strategies contained herein may not be suitable for your situation. You should consult with a professional where appropriate. Neither the publisher nor author shall be liable for any loss of profit or any other commercial damages, including but not limited to special, incidental, consequential, or other damages.

This publication is designed to provide accurate and authoritative information in regard to the subject matter covered. It is sold with the understanding that the publisher is not engaged in rendering professional services. If legal, accounting, medical, psychological or any other expert assistance is required, the services of a competent professional person should be sought.

Designations used by companies to distinguish their products are often claimed as trademarks. In all instances where John Wiley & Sons, Inc. is aware of a claim, the product names appear in initial capital or all capital letters. Readers, however, should contact the appropriate companies for more complete information regarding trademarks and registration.

For general information on our other products and services please contact our Customer Care Department within the United States at (800) 762-2974, outside the United States at (317) 572-3993 or fax (317) 572-4002.

Wiley publishes in a variety of print and electronic formats and by print-on-demand. Some material included with standard print versions of this book may not be included in e-books or in print-on-demand. If this book refers to media such as a CD or DVD that is not included in the version you purchased, you may download this material at http://booksupport.wiley.com. For more information about Wiley products, visit www.wiley.com.

ISBN: 978-0-470-56846-0

Printed in the United States of America

10 9 8 7 6 5 4 3 2

# Contents

Introduction ... vii

Chapter 1  What Is Bipolar Disorder? ... 1

Chapter 2  What Are the Six Steps in Building a Treatment Plan? ... 7

Chapter 3  What Is the Brief History of the Empirically Supported Treatments Movement? ... 9

Chapter 4  What Are the Identified Empirically Supported Treatments for Bipolar Disorder? ... 14

Chapter 5  How Do You Integrate Empirically Supported Treatments Into Treatment Planning? ... 23

Closing Remarks and Resources ... 50

Appendix A  A Sample Evidence-Based Treatment Plan for Bipolar Disorder ... 52

Appendix B  Chapter Review Test Questions and Answers Explained ... 55

# Introduction

This *Facilitator's Guide* is designed to help you lead an educational training session in *Evidence-Based Treatment Planning for Bipolar Disorder*. It is to be used in conjunction with the DVD and its *Companion Workbook*. The *Guide* walks you through the process of delivering a training session.

The training session should be conducted in a comfortable room, where participants can read and write in their workbooks. A DVD player and monitor are required.

## Organization

In this *Guide* you will find in each chapter:

- Chapter review questions and answers
- Chapter review test questions and answers
- Talking points—this feature presents an optional question with a highlighted point or points to include in the discussion.
- Chapter references

In appropriate chapters the references are divided into those for *empirical support*, those for *clinical resources*, and those for *bibliotherapy resources*. Empirical support references are selected studies or reviews of the empirical work supporting the efficacy of the empirically supported treatments (ESTs) discussed in the chapter. The clinical resources are books, manuals, or other resources for clinicians that describe the application, or "how to," of the treatments discussed. The bibliotherapy resources are selected publications and Web sites relevant to the DVD content that may be helpful to clinicians, clients, or laypersons.

Examples of client homework are included at www.wiley.com/go/bpdwb. They are designed to enhance understanding of therapeutic interventions, in addition to being potentially useful clinically.

Appendix A contains an example of an evidence-based treatment plan for Bipolar Disorder, Depression. In Appendix B, correct and incorrect answers to all chapter review test questions are explained.

## Chapter Points

This DVD is electronically marked with chapter points that delineate the beginning of major sections throughout the program. You may skip to any one of these chapter points on the DVD by clicking on the forward arrow. The chapter points for this program are as follows:

➤ Defining Bipolar Disorder
➤ Six Steps in Building a Psychotherapy Treatment Plan
➤ Brief History of the EST Movement
➤ ESTs for Bipolar Disorder
➤ Integrating ESTs for Bipolar Disorder Into a Treatment Plan
➤ An Evidence-Based Treatment Plan for Bipolar Disorder

## Series Rationale

Evidence-based practice (EBP) is steadily becoming the standard of mental health care as it has in medical health care. Borrowing from the Institute of Medicine's definition (Institute of Medicine, 2001), the American Psychological Association (APA) has defined EBP as "the integration of the best available research with clinical expertise in the context of patient characteristics, culture, and preferences" (American Psychological Association Presidential Task Force on Evidence-Based Practice (APA), 2006).

Professional organizations such as the American Psychological Association, the National Association of Social Workers, and the American Psychiatric Association, as well as consumer organizations such the National Alliance for the Mentally Ill (NAMI), are endorsing EBP. At the federal level, a major joint initiative of the National Institute of Mental Health and Department of Health and Human Services' Substance Abuse and Mental Health Services Administration (SAMHSA) focuses on promoting, implementing, and evaluating evidence-based mental health programs and practices within state mental health systems (APA, 2006). In some practice settings, EBP is even becoming mandated. It is clear that the call for evidence-based practice is being increasingly sounded.

Unfortunately, many mental health care providers cannot or do not stay abreast of results from clinical research and how they can inform their practices. Although it has rightfully been argued that the relevance of some research to the clinician's needs is weak, there are products of clinical research whose efficacy has been well established and whose effectiveness in the community setting has received support. Clinicians and clinicians-in-training interested in empirically informing their treatments could benefit from educational programs that make this goal more easily attainable.

This series of DVDs and companion workbooks is designed to introduce clinicians and students to the process of empirically informing their psychotherapy treatment plans. The series begins with an introduction to the efforts to identify research-supported treatments and how the products of these efforts can be used to inform treatment planning. The other programs in the series focus on empirically informed treatment planning for each of several commonly seen clinical problems. In each problem-focused DVD, issues involved in defining or diagnosing the presenting problem are reviewed. Research-supported treatments for the problem are described, as well as the process used to identify them. Viewers are then systematically guided through the process of creating a treatment plan, and shown how the plan can be informed by goals, objectives, and interventions consistent with those of the identified research-supported treatments. Example vignettes of selected interventions are also provided.

This series is intended to be educational and informative in nature and not meant to be a substitute for clinical training in the specific interventions discussed and demonstrated. References to empirical support of the treatments described, clinical resource material, and training opportunities are provided.

# Presenters

*Dr. Art Jongsma* is the Series Editor and co-author of the Practice*Planners*® series published by John Wiley & Sons. He has authored or co-authored more than

## Exhibit I.1 Dr. Tim Bruce and Dr. Art Jongsma

40 books in this series. Among the books included in this series are the highly regarded *The Complete Adult Psychotherapy Treatment Planner*, *The Adolescent* and *The Child Psychotherapy Treatment Planners*, and *The Addiction Treatment Planner*. All of these books, along with *The Severe and Persistent Mental Illness Treatment Planner*, *The Family Therapy Treatment Planner*, *The Couples Psychotherapy Treatment Planner*, *The Older Adult Psychotherapy Treatment Planner*, and *The Veterans and Active Duty Military Psychotherapy Treatment Planner*, are informed with Objectives and Interventions that are supported by research evidence.

Dr. Jongsma also created the clinical record management software tool Thera*Scribe*®, which uses point-and-click technology to easily develop, store, and print treatment plans, progress notes, and homework assignments. He has conducted treatment planning and software training workshops for mental health professionals around the world.

Dr. Jongsma's clinical career began as a psychologist in a large private psychiatric hospital. After working in the hospital for about 10 years, he then transitioned to outpatient work in his own private practice clinic, Psychological Consultants, in Grand Rapids, Michigan, for 25 years. He has been writing best-selling books and software for mental health professionals since 1995. He lives in a suburb of Grand Rapids with his wife, Judy.

*Dr. Timothy Bruce* is a Professor and Associate Chair of the Department of Psychiatry and Behavioral Medicine at the University of Illinois, College of Medicine in Peoria, Illinois, where he also directs medical student education. He is a licensed clinical psychologist who completed his graduate training at SUNY-Albany under the mentorship of Dr. David Barlow and his residency training at Wilford Hall Medical Center under the direction of Dr. Robert Klepac. In addition to maintaining an active clinical practice at the university, Dr. Bruce has written numerous publications, including books, professional journal articles, book chapters, and professional educational materials, many on the topic of evidence-based practice. Most recently, he has served as the developmental editor empirically informing Dr. Jongsma's best-selling Practice*Planners*® series.

Dr. Bruce is also Executive Director of the Center for the Dissemination of Evidence-Based Mental Health Practices, a state- and federally funded initiative to disseminate evidence-based psychological and pharmacological practices across Illinois. Highly recognized as an educator, Dr. Bruce has received nearly thirty awards for his teaching of students and professionals during his career.

# References

American Psychological Association Presidential Task Force on Evidence-Based Practice. (2006). Evidence-based practice in psychology. *American Psychologist, 61*, 271–285.

Berghuis, D., Jongsma, A., & Bruce, T. (2006). *The severe and persistent mental illness treatment planner* (2nd ed.). Hoboken, NJ: Wiley.

Dattilio, F., Jongsma, A., & Davis, S. (2009). *The family therapy treatment planner* (2nd ed.). Hoboken, NJ: Wiley.

Institute of Medicine. (2001). *Crossing the quality chasm: A new health system for the 21st century*. Washington, DC: National Academy Press.

Jongsma, A., Peterson, M., & Bruce, T. (2006). *The complete adult psychotherapy treatment planner* (4th ed.). Hoboken, NJ: Wiley.

Jongsma, A., Peterson, M., McInnis, W., & Bruce, T. (2006a). *The adolescent psychotherapy treatment planner* (4th ed.). Hoboken, NJ: Wiley.

Jongsma, A., Peterson, M., McInnis, W., & Bruce, T. (2006b). *The child psychotherapy treatment planner* (4th ed.). Hoboken, NJ: Wiley.

Moore, B., and Jongsma, A. (2009). *The veterans and active duty military psychotherapy treatment planner*. Hoboken, NJ: Wiley.

Perkinson, R., Jongsma, A., & Bruce, T. (2009). *The addiction treatment planner* (4th ed.). Hoboken, NJ: Wiley.

# CHAPTER 1

# What Is Bipolar Disorder?

## Chapter Review

1. How are mood disorders diagnosed?

   In diagnosing mood disorders such as bipolar disorder, the first step is to assess for any current or past mood episodes. This information is then used to make the diagnosis of a mood disorder.

2. What are the different mood episodes that are used to make a diagnosis of a mood disorder?

   A mood episode is a cluster of specific mood symptoms that have an onset, occur over a period of time, and represent a change from normal functioning. Below, the four types of mood episodes that are used to make the diagnosis of a mood disorder are presented.

---

### Four Types of Mood Episodes

- Major Depressive
- Manic
- Hypomanic
- Mixed

---

3. What are the features of each of the mood episodes?

### The Major Depressive Episode

A useful acronym for remembering the features of a major depressive episode is SIGECAPSS, where each letter of the word stands for a specific diagnostic characteristic of the episode.

## What Is Bipolar Disorder?

> **Features of a Major Depressive Episode (SIGECAPSS)**
> 
> **S**adness
> **I**nterest
> **G**uilt
> **E**nergy
> **C**oncentration
> **A**ppetite
> **P**sychomotor
> **S**leep
> **S**uicidality

In this acronym, the first S stands for the mood symptom, which is typically sadness, but may be irritability. The I stands for loss of interest, also known as *anhedonia*. In addition, there may be guilt (G), referring to the broader concept of low self-worth or self-esteem, self-loathing, and the like; the E represents loss of energy or fatigue; C stands for cognitive deficits such as concentration, attention, or decision-making abilities; a loss or gain of weight or appetite is symbolized by the A; the P stands for psychomotor behavior and/or speech, which is often retarded or slow in depression; the next S stands for a sleep disturbance involving insomnia or hypersomnia; and, finally, the last S stands for suicidality, ranging from suicidal thoughts only to a serious suicide attempt.

A major depressive episode is characterized by the presence of at least five of these symptoms, occurring most of the day, nearly every day, for at least two weeks, and representing a change from previous functioning. It's important to note that at least one of the five symptoms must be either a depressed (or irritable) mood (represented by the first S in the acronym) or a loss of interest (represented by the I).

### The Manic Episode

On the other end of the polar spectrum from depression is the manic episode. It is characterized by a distinct period of abnormally and persistently elevated, expansive, or irritable mood, lasting at least one week (or any duration if hospitalization is necessary). During this period of mood disturbance, three (or more) of the following symptoms have persisted (four if the mood is only irritable) and have been present to a significant degree.

---

### Features of a Manic Episode

- Inflated self-esteem or grandiosity
- Decreased need for sleep
- More talkative than usual or pressure to keep talking
- Flight of ideas or the subjective experience that thoughts are racing
- Distractibility
- Increased goal-directed activity or psychomotor agitation
- Excessive involvement in pleasurable, high-risk behavior

---

The manic episode must be sufficiently severe to cause marked impairment in occupational functioning or in usual social activities or relationships. Or, the episode may necessitate hospitalization to prevent harm to self or others. Or, there are psychotic features, such as delusions of grandeur or severe thought disorganization.

### The Hypomanic Episode

A hypomanic episode represents a less severe form of mania. For example, although the diagnostic criteria require a distinct period of persistently elevated, expansive, or irritable mood, it is not "abnormally" so as noted in the criteria for mania, and need last throughout only four days (as opposed to one week with mania). And although the criteria for a hypomanic episode have the same number and types of symptoms as the manic episode, this type of mood disturbance is not severe enough to cause marked impairment in social or occupational functioning or to necessitate hospitalization, and there are no psychotic features. Instead, the episode represents a change in mood and functioning that is observable to others and is uncharacteristic of the person when not symptomatic. Key features of hypomania are summarized below.

---

### Features of a Hypomanic Episode

- Same symptoms as mania
- Symptoms less severe than mania
- Symptoms need last only four days, not seven as in mania
- Not severe enough to cause marked impairment or hospitalization
- No psychotic features

---

### The Mixed Episode

Lastly, a mixed episode represents a highly unstable and severe shifting of mood. In it, the criteria are met both for a manic episode and for a major depressive episode nearly every day during at least a one-week period. In addition, and like a manic episode, the mood disturbance is sufficiently severe to cause marked impairment in occupational functioning, social activities or relationships, or to necessitate hospitalization, or there are psychotic features. Criteria for a Mixed Episode are summarized below.

---

#### Mixed Episode Criteria

The criteria are met both for a manic episode and for a major depressive episode (except for duration) nearly every day during at least a one-week period.

The mood disturbance is sufficiently severe to cause marked impairment in occupational functioning, social activities, or relationships with others, or to necessitate hospitalization to prevent harm to self or others, or there are psychotic features.

---

As with all mental disorders, the symptoms of any of these four types of mood episodes are not due to the direct physiological effects of a substance (e.g., a drug of abuse, a medication, or other treatment), or a general medical condition (e.g., hyper- or hypothyroidism).

4. What are the mood disorders?

### Mood Disorders

Once past and present mood episodes have been assessed, they are then used to make the diagnosis of a mood disorder. In the *DSM*, mood disorders may be bipolar, meaning that there has been or currently is evidence of a manic, hypomanic, or mixed episode in the clinical picture. Or, they may be unipolar, meaning that there is evidence of one or more depressive episodes or depressive symptoms, but without any current or past manic, hypomanic, or mixed episodes. Major Depressive Disorder and a chronic lower-level state of depression called Dysthymic Disorder are the Unipolar Mood Disorders. There are three Bipolar Mood Disorders: Bipolar I, Bipolar II, and a chronic lower-level mood disturbance called Cyclothymia.

---

#### Bipolar Mood Disorders

- Bipolar Disorder I
- Bipolar Disorder II
- Cyclothymia

The essential feature of Bipolar I Disorder is a clinical course that is characterized by the occurrence of one or more manic episodes or mixed episodes. Individuals often have also had one or more major depressive episodes.

---

### Bipolar I Disorder Criteria

- One or more manic episodes or mixed episodes
- May have had one or more major depressive episodes, but this is not required for the diagnosis

---

Bipolar II Disorder is characterized by one or more past or present major depressive episodes as well as at least one past or present hypomanic episode. In addition, there has never been a manic episode or a mixed episode in the clinical picture, something that, if it occurred, would change the diagnosis to Bipolar I.

---

### Bipolar II Disorder Criteria

- One or more major depressive episodes, with at least one hypomanic episode
- Never been a manic episode or a mixed episode

---

5. What are the lifetime prevalence, gender distribution, and average age of onset of bipolar disorder?

## Epidemiology of Bipolar Disorder

Bipolar disorder occurs in approximately 1% of the population, and it is seen equally across men and women. The average age of onset is 20. In men, the first episode is more likely to be manic, whereas in women, it's more likely to be depressive. In men, the number of manic episodes to depressive episodes is typically equal or greater, whereas in women, depressive episodes typically predominate. Bipolar disorder is a recurrent disorder, in which subsequent episodes are seen in more than 90% of those experiencing their first episode. Selected epidemiological information for Bipolar Disorder is summarized below.

---

### Epidemiology of Bipolar Disorder

- Lifetime prevalence: 1% (.4–1.6)
- Gender distribution: 50/50
- Average age of onset: 20
- Bipolar disorder is a recurrent disorder

## Chapter Review Test Questions

1. A 22-year-old male presents to his family physician with pervasive sadness, loss of appetite, and sleeplessness for three weeks. He complains of feeling tired and has difficulty concentrating on his schoolwork. He has dropped out of activities with friends that he previously enjoyed. His physician has ruled out medical and substance etiologies and is considering the diagnosis of Major Depressive Disorder (MDD). To determine if this is the correct mood disorder diagnosis, which of the following does the physician need to do?

   A. Assess for an abuse history
   B. Assess for past mood episodes
   C. Assess the past treatment history
   D. Explore the family history of mood disorders

   Answer: B

2. True or False: A person with a diagnosis of a mood disorder may find that the diagnosis could accurately change over time (e.g., be one diagnosis a year ago and another currently).

   True.

---

**Talking Point**

The process of diagnosing mood disorders differs from that of other mental disorders in that one must first assess for past and present mood episodes (i.e., manic, hypomanic, mixed, and depressive) and then use that information to make the diagnosis of a mood disorder (e.g., major depressive disorder, bipolar disorder). Consider facilitating a discussion about this process and the importance of assessing past episodes. For example, you might ask, "Why does the presence of a current depressive episode not necessarily warrant the diagnosis of Major Depressive Disorder?"

- The answer, of course, is that depression can occur in the context of a bipolar disorder, so the diagnostician must assess current and *past* episodes before deciding the appropriate mood disorder. More discussion of this diagnostic process could ensue with other mood disorders.

---

## Chapter Reference

American Psychiatric Association. (2000). *Diagnostic and statistical manual of mental disorders* (4th ed., text rev.). Washington, DC: American Psychiatric Association.

CHAPTER 2

# What Are the Six Steps in Building a Treatment Plan?

## Chapter Review

1. What are the six steps involved in developing a psychotherapy treatment plan?

---

**Six Steps in Building a Psychotherapy Treatment Plan**

Step 1: Identify primary and secondary problems
Step 2: Describe the problem's behavioral manifestations (symptom pattern)
Step 3: Make a diagnosis based on *DSM/ICD* criteria
Step 4: Specify long-term goals
Step 5: Create short-term objectives
Step 6: Select therapeutic interventions

---

**Key Point**

One important aspect of effective treatment planning is that each plan should be tailored to the individual client's particular problems and needs. Treatment plans should not be boilerplate, even if clients have similar problems. Consistent with the definition of an evidence-based practice, the individual's strengths and weaknesses, unique stressors, cultural and social network, family circumstances, and symptom patterns must be considered in developing a treatment strategy. Clinicians should rely on their own good clinical judgment and plan a treatment that is appropriate for the distinctive individual with whom they are working.

## Chapter Review Test Questions

1. As noted previously, some patients with bipolar disorder may show grandiose delusions, while others may not. Some may be engaging in several high-risk behaviors, while others may not. In which step of treatment planning would you record the particular expressions of bipolar disorder for your individual client?

    A. Creating short-term objectives
    B. Describing the problem's manifestations
    C. Identifying the primary problem
    D. Selecting treatment interventions
    Answer: B

2. The statement "Learn and implement problem-solving skills to manage problems and reduce the risk of mood episodes" is an example of a statement describing which of the following elements of a psychotherapy treatment plan?

    A. A primary problem
    B. A short-term objective
    C. A symptom manifestation
    D. A treatment intervention
    Answer: B

---

### Talking Point

What is the relationship between short-term objectives (STOs) and treatment interventions (TIs) in a psychotherapy treatment plan?

- In short, STOs are desired actions of the client, while TIs are the therapist's actions designed to help clients achieve their objectives.

CHAPTER 3

# What Is the Brief History of the Empirically Supported Treatments Movement?

## Chapter Review

1. How did Division 12 of the APA identify ESTs?

---

### Process Used to Identify ESTs

Task group reviewers evaluated the psychotherapy outcome literature to identify treatments whose efficacy had been supported through empirical study. Two primary sets of criteria were used to judge the evidence base supporting any particular therapy. One was termed well-established, the other probably efficacious.

---

2. What are the primary differences between *well-established* and *probably efficacious* criteria used to identify ESTs?

---

- The criteria for a well-established treatment required at least two randomized, placebo-controlled trials (RCT), or two randomized trials comparing the treatment to an already established treatment, or a large series of single-case design studies. In these studies, treatment manuals had to be used, and characteristics of the client sample had to be specified. Finally, replication by independent investigators had to have been demonstrated.
- The criteria for a probably efficacious treatment could be met with two demonstrations of efficacy over a wait-list control. This is a lower level of evidence than for a well-established treatment in that it rules out only that the condition being treated does not remit on its own.
- Alternatively, one or more randomized, placebo-controlled trials or randomized trials comparing the treatment to an already established treatment in which manuals were used, client characteristics were specified, but independent replication had *not* been demonstrated would suffice.
- As with the well-established criteria, a single case series, but of smaller size than that required for well-established, could be used.

---

See Figure 3.1 for use if more detailed questions arise.

## Figure 3.1

*Specific Criteria for Well-Established and Probably Efficacious Treatments*

### Criteria for a Well-Established Treatment

For a psychological treatment to be considered *well-established*, the evidence base supporting it had to be characterized by the following:

I. At least two good between-group design experiments demonstrating efficacy in one or more of the following ways:
   A. Superior (statistically significantly so) to pill or psychological placebo or to another treatment.
   B. Equivalent to an already established treatment in experiments with adequate sample sizes.

OR

II. A large series of single-case design experiments (n > 9) demonstrating efficacy. These experiments must have:
   A. Used good experimental designs
   B. Compared the intervention to another treatment as in IA

**Further Criteria for Both I and II:**
III. Experiments must be conducted with treatment manuals.
IV. Characteristics of the client samples must be clearly specified.
V. Effects must have been demonstrated by at least two different investigators or investigating teams.

### Criteria for a Probably Efficacious Treatment

For a psychological treatment to be considered *probably efficacious*, the evidence base supporting it had to meet the following criteria:

I. Two experiments showing the treatment is superior (statistically significantly so) to a waiting-list control group

OR

II. One or more experiments meeting the Well-Established Treatment Criteria IA or IB, III, and IV, but not V

OR

III. A small series of single-case design experiments (n > 3) otherwise meeting Well-Established Treatment

---

Adapted from "Update on Empirically Validated Therapies, II," by D. L. Chambless, M. J. Baker, D. H. Baucom, L. E. Beutler, K. S. Calhoun, P. Crits-Christoph, . . . S. R. Woody, 1998, *The Clinical Psychologist, 51*(1), 3–16.

> **Key Point**
>
> Division 12's criteria for a well-established treatment are similar to the standards used by the United States Food and Drug Administration (FDA) to evaluate the safety and efficacy of proposed medications. The FDA requires demonstration that a proposed medication is significantly superior to a nonspecific control treatment (a pill placebo) in at least two randomized controlled trials conducted by independent research groups. Division 12's criteria for a well-established treatment require the equivalent of this standard as well as other features relevant to judging a psychological treatment's efficacy (e.g., a clear description of the treatment and study participants). By extension, if the FDA were to evaluate psychotherapies using the criteria they use for medication, it would allow sale of those judged to be well-established.

3. Where can information about ESTs and evidence-based practices be found?

- The Society of Clinical Psychology, Division 12, maintains the growing list of research-supported psychological treatments at: http://www.psychologicaltreatments.org
- Descriptions of the treatments identified through many of the early EST reviews, as well as references to the empirical work supporting them, clinical resources, and training opportunities, can be found at www.therapyadvisor.com. This resource was developed by Personal Improvement Computer Systems (PICS) with funding from the National Institute of Mental Health and in consultation with members of the original Division 12 task groups. Information found on Therapyadvisor is provided by the primary author/researcher(s) of the given EST.
- Great Britain is at the forefront of the effort to identify evidence-based treatments and develop guidelines for practice. The latest products of their work can be found at the Web site for the National Institute for Health and Clinical Excellence (NICE): www.nice.org.uk.
- The Substance Abuse and Mental Health Services Administration (SAMHSA) has an initiative to evaluate, identify, and provide information on various mental health practices. Their work, entitled "The National Registry of Evidence-based Programs and Practices or NREPP," can be found online at www.nrepp.samhsa.gov.
- The Agency for Health Care Policy and Research, now called the Agency for Healthcare Research and Quality (AHRQ), has established guidelines and criteria for identifying evidence-based practices and provides links to evidence-based clinical practice guidelines for various medical and mental health problems at www.ahrq.gov/clinic/epcix.htm.
- The Cochrane Collaboration is an international network of professionals who conduct systematic reviews of research in human health care and health policy. Among their products are critical reviews of psychological treatment interventions and specific intervention questions. They can be found on the Web at www.cochrane.org.
- Other reviews can be found in the reference section of Chapter 4 under "Empirical Support."

## Chapter Review Test Questions

1. Which statement best describes the process used to identify ESTs?
   A. Consumers of mental health services nominated therapies.
   B. Experts came to a consensus based on their experiences with the treatments.
   C. Researchers submitted their works.
   D. Task groups reviewed the literature using clearly defined selection criteria for ESTs.

   Answer: D

2. Based on the differences in their criteria, in which of the following ways are *well-established* treatments different from those classified as *probably efficacious*?
   A. Only *probably efficacious* allowed the use of a single-case design experiment.
   B. Only *well-established* allowed studies comparing the treatment to a psychological placebo.
   C. Only *well-established* required demonstration by at least two different, independent investigators or investigating teams.
   D. Only *well-established* allowed studies comparing the treatment to a pill placebo.

   Answer: C

---

**Talking Points**

Why would it be important to have a treatment effect demonstrated by at least two different investigators or investigating teams (i.e., independently replicated)?

- You can discuss sources of bias and confounds that may influence the outcome of a psychotherapy.
- In particular, consider discussing factors in some studies that can lead to *allegiance effects*, in which the positive outcome is found only by investigators who are, generally speaking, advocates of the therapy. Examples could include demand characteristics, advanced training in the techniques, and biased assessment of response.

---

## Chapter References

Chambless, D. L., & Ollendick, T. H. (2001). Empirically supported psychological interventions: Controversies and evidence. *Annual Review of Psychology, 52*, 685–716.

Chambless, D. L., Sanderson, W. C., Shoham, V., Bennett Johnson, S., Pope, K. S., Crits-Christoph, P., . . . McCurry, S. (1996). An update on empirically validated therapies. *The Clinical Psychologist, 49*, 5–18.

Chambless, D. L., Baker, M. J., Baucom, D. H., Beutler, L. E., Calhoun, K. S., Crits-Christoph, P., . . . Woody, S. R. (1998). Update on empirically validated therapies, II. *The Clinical Psychologist, 51,* 3–16.

Gatz, M., Fiske, A., Fox, L. S., Kaskie, B., Kasl-Godley, J. E., McCallum, T., & Wetherell, J. (1998). Empirically validated psychological treatments for older adults. *Journal of Mental Health and Aging, 41,* 9–46.

Kendall, P. C., & Chambless, D. L. (Eds.). (1998). Empirically supported psychological therapies [special issue]. *Journal of Consulting and Clinical Psychology, 66*(3), 151–162.

Lonigan, C. J., & Elbert, J. C. (Eds.). (1998). Empirically supported psychosocial interventions for children [special issue]. *Journal of Clinical Child Psychology, 27,* 138–226.

Miklowitz, D. J. (2008). Adjunctive psychotherapy for bipolar disorder: State of the evidence. *American Journal of Psychiatry, 165,* 1408–1419.

Nathan, P. E., & Gorman, J. M. (Eds.). (2007). *A guide to treatments that work* (3rd ed.). New York, NY: Oxford University Press.

Spirito, A. (Ed.). (1999). Empirically supported treatments in pediatric psychology [special issue]. *Journal of Pediatric Psychology, 24,* 87–174.

# CHAPTER 4

# What Are the Identified Empirically Supported Treatments for Bipolar Disorder?

## Chapter Review

1. What are the research-supported treatments for bipolar disorders discussed in this chapter?

---

**ESTs for Bipolar Disorder from Division 12 of APA**

FOR MANIA:
- Well-Established:
    - Systematic Care
    - Group Psychoeducation
- Probably Efficacious
    - Cognitive-Behavioral Therapy

FOR BIPOLAR DEPRESSION:
- Well-Established
    - Family-Focused Therapy
- Probably Efficacious
    - Interpersonal and Social Rhythm Therapy
    - Cognitive-Behavioral Therapy

---

2. What are the primary emphases, features, or components of each of the ESTs for bipolar disorder?

## Group Psychoeducational Emphases

- Bipolar disorder and its features
- Biological factors in its etiology
- Psychosocial factors
- Relapse prevention skills
- Regulating activity
- Communication skills
- Problem-solving skills
- Development of a personal care plan

## Features Of Systematic Care

- Outpatient treatment is specialized
- Evidence-based pharmacotherapy algorithm is applied
- Group psychoeducation is conducted
- Psychiatric care is coordinated by a nurse
- Patient's response to treatment is monitored via telephone contact
- Monitoring information is fed back to the psychiatrists to inform their medication decision making
- Nurse coordinators make additional telephone contacts to provide general support, encourage
- group participation, facilitate in-person follow-up care, and offer crisis management
- The group psychoeducation program consists of five weekly sessions followed by twice-monthly
- sessions for up to three years

## Components of CBT for Mania

- Psychoeducation
- Cognitive restructuring
- Lifestyle/activity stabilization
- Regulating sleep patterns
- Various behavioral techniques (e.g., skills training, stimulus control)

## Primary Components Of FFT

- Psychoeducation
- Communication enhancement training
- Problem-solving skills training

## Primary Emphases of IPSRT for Bipolar Depression

- Resolving key interpersonal problems
- Stabilizing social rhythms through activity regulation
- Sleep/wake cycles
- Timing of daily routines
- Balance social stimulation

3. What themes emerge from this literature that might represent a set of evidence-based practices for bipolar disorder?

---

### Themes Across Evidence-Based Psychological Treatments for Bipolar Disorder

- Educate patients and family about the illness
- When appropriate, treat family members or significant others to reduce conflict and negative expressed emotion in the family system and develop social support
- Improve medication/therapy adherence
- Teach patients to monitor mood and activity state/level of stimulation
- Modify maladaptive beliefs/cognitive vulnerabilities that predispose patients to severe depressive or manic episodes
- Address maladaptive perceptions, judgments, behaviors
- Assist patients in problem solving and relevant coping strategies to reduce the impact of aversive life events
- Assist in stabilizing lifestyle, social routines, and sleep
- Develop coping plans to prevent or minimize relapses
- Develop a relapse prevention plan

---

### Talking Points

It was mentioned in this chapter that outcomes of psychotherapies may differ in that some seem more effective for mania and others for depression, generally speaking. Consider facilitating a discussion as to why that might be.

- In launching and facilitating this discussion, it may be helpful to keep in mind the observation by Miklowitz (2008). He pointed out that manic symptoms are most consistently associated with medication nonadherence, life events that promote goal striving, and sleep/wake cycle disruption. Accordingly, interventions that focus on the early identification of prodromal (or pre-episode) symptoms (such as sleep changes), as well as compliance with medications, are more effective with manic than depressive symptoms. Examples include psychoeducation and CBT.
- In contrast, patient- and family-centered approaches that focus on skills for managing interpersonal or familial relationships—such as communication and problem-solving strategies or interpersonal therapy—appear to be more effective for depressive than manic symptoms.

## Chapter Review Test Questions

1. According to APA's Division 12, The Society of Clinical Psychology, which of the following has met their criteria for a well-established psychological treatment for bipolar depression?

    A. Cognitive-behavioral therapy (CBT)
    B. Interpersonal and social rhythm therapy (IPSRT)
    C. Family-focused therapy (FFT)
    D. Group psychoeducation (GP)

    Answer: C

2. Which of the following best describes the outcome of the Systematic Treatment Enhancement Program for Bipolar Disorder (STEP-BD) study, in which cognitive-behavioral therapy (CBT), interpersonal and social rhythm therapy (IPSRT), and family-focused therapy (FBT) were compared to a control psychological treatment while all participants were also on medication?

    A. CBT was associated with a faster recovery rate from acute depression than all other treatments.
    B. CBT, FFT, and IPSRT were all associated with a faster recovery rate from acute depression than the control treatment.
    C. FFT was associated with a faster recovery rate from acute depression than all other treatments.
    D. IPSRT was associated with a faster recovery rate from acute depression than all other treatments.

    Answer: B

## Selected Chapter References

### General and Review

American Psychological Association Presidential Task Force on Evidence-Based Practice. (2006). Evidence-based practice in psychology. *American Psychologist, 61*(4), 271–185.

Institute of Medicine. (2001). *Crossing the quality chasm: A new health system for the 21st century.* Washington, DC: National Academy Press.

Miklowitz, D. J. (2008). Adjunctive psychotherapy for bipolar disorder: State of the evidence. *American Journal of Psychiatry, 165,* 1408–1419.

Miklowitz, D. J., & Craighead, W. E. (2007). Psychological treatments for bipolar disorder. In P. E. Nathan & J. M. Gorman (Eds.), *A guide to treatments that work* (pp. 309–322). New York, NY: Oxford University Press.

Reiser, R. P., & Thompson, L. W. (2005). *Bipolar disorder.* Cambridge, MA: Hogrefe.

## For Psychoeducation
### Empirical Support
Colom, F., Vieta, E., Martinez-Aran, A., Reinares, M., Goikolea, J. M., Benabarre, A., ... & Corominas, J. (2003). A randomized trial on the efficacy of group psychoeducation in the prophylaxis of recurrences in bipolar patients whose disease is in remission. *Archives of General Psychiatry, 60,* 402–407.

Colom, F., Vieta, E., Sanchez-Moreno, J., Martinez-Aran, A., Reinares, M., Goikolea, J. M., ... & Scott, J. (2005). Stabilizing the stabilizer: Group psychoeducation enhances the stability of serum lithium levels. *Bipolar Disorders, 7,* 32–36.

Colom, F., Vieta, E., Reinares, M., Martinez-Aran, A., Torrent, C., Goikolea, J. M., ... Gasto, C. (2003). Psychoeducation efficacy in bipolar disorders: Beyond compliance enhancement. *Journal of Clinical Psychiatry, 64,* 1101–1105.

Perry, A., Tarrier, N., Morriss, R., McCarthy, E., & Limb, K. (1999). Randomised controlled trial of efficacy of teaching patients with bipolar disorder to identify early symptoms of relapse and obtain treatment. *British Medical Journal, 318,* 149–153.

### Clinical Resources
Colom, F., & Vieta, E. (2006). *Psychoeducation manual for bipolar disorder.* New York, NY: Cambridge University Press.

## For Systematic Care
### Empirical Support
Bauer, M. S., McBride, L., Williford, W. O., Glick, H., Kinosian, B., Altshuler, L., ... Sajatovic, M. (2006). Collaborative care for bipolar disorder, Part II: Impact on clinical outcome, function, and costs. *Psychiatric Services, 57,* 937–945.

Simon, G. E., Ludman, E. J., Bauer, M. S., Unutzer, J., & Operskalski, B. (2006). Long-term effectiveness and cost of a systematic care program for bipolar disorder. *Archives of General Psychiatry, 63,* 500–508.

Simon, G. E., Ludman, E. J., Unutzer, J., Bauer, M. S., Operskalski, B., & Rutter, C. (2005). Randomized trial of a population-based care program for people with bipolar disorder. *Psychological Medicine, 35,* 13–24.

### Clinical Resources
Bauer, M. S., & McBride, L. (2003). *Structured group psychotherapy for bipolar disorder: The life goals program* (2nd ed.). New York, NY: Springer.

### Training Opportunities
Mark S. Bauer, M.D., Brockton Division, VA Boston Healthcare System, Brockton, MA, Mark.Bauer@va.gov.

# For Cognitive-Behavioral Therapy

## Empirical Support

Ball, J. R., Mitchell, P. B., Corry, J. C., Skillecorn, A., Smith, M., & Malhi, G. S. (2006). A randomized controlled trial of cognitive therapy for bipolar disorder: Focus on long-term change. *Journal of Clinical Psychiatry, 67*, 277–286.

Lam, D. H., Hayward, P., Watkins, E. R., Wright, K., & Sham, P. (2005). Relapse prevention in patients with bipolar disorder: Cognitive therapy outcome after 2 years. *American Journal of Psychiatry, 162*, 324–329.

Lam, D. H., McCrone, P., Wright, K., & Kerr. N. (2005). Cost-effectiveness of relapse-prevention cognitive therapy for bipolar disorder: 30-month study. *British Journal of Psychiatry, 186*, 400–506.

Lam, D. H., Watkins, E. R., Hayward, P., Bright, J., Wright, K., Kerr, N., . . . Sham, P. (2003). A randomized controlled study of cognitive therapy of relapse prevention for bipolar affective disorder: Outcome of the first year. *Archives of General Psychiatry, 60*, 145–152.

Miklowitz, D. J., Otto, M. W., Frank, E., Reilly-Harrington, N. A., Kogan, J. N., Sachs, G. S., . . . & Wisniewski, S. R. (2007). Intensive psychosocial intervention enhances functioning in patients with bipolar depression: Results from a 9-month randomized controlled trial. *American Journal of Psychiatry, 164*, 1340–1347.

Patelis-Siotis, I., Young, T. L., Robb, J. C., Marriott, M., Bieling, P. J., Cox, L. C., . . . Joffe, R. T. (2001). Group cognitive behavioral therapy for bipolar disorder: A feasibility and effectiveness study. *Journal of Affective Disorders, 65*, 145–153.

Scott, J., Paykel, E., Morriss, R., Bental, R., Kinderman, P., Johnson, T., . . . Hayhurst, H. (2006). Cognitive behavioural therapy for severe and recurrent bipolar disorders: A randomised controlled trial. *British Journal of Psychiatry, 188*, 313–320.

Zaretsky, A., Lancee, W., Miller, C., Harris, A., & Parikh, S. V. (2008). Is cognitive behavioural therapy more effective than psychoeducation in bipolar disorder? *Canadian Journal of Psychiatry, 53*, 441–448.

## Clinical Resources

Lam, D. H., Jones, S. H., Hayward, P., & Bright, J. A. (1999). *Cognitive therapy for bipolar disorder: A therapist's guide to concepts, methods, and practice.* West Sussex, England: Wiley Press.

Otto, M. W., Reilly-Harrington, N., & Sachs, G. S. (2003) Psychoeducational and cognitive-behavioral strategies in the management of bipolar disorder. *Journal of Affective Disorders, 73*, 171–181.

### Training Opportunities

Dominic Lam, University of Hull, Holly House, Welton Old Road, Welton, Brough, North Humber HU15 1HU, Tel: 01482 669310.

## For Family-Focused Therapy

### Empirical Support

Clarkin, J. F., Carpenter, D., Hull, J., Wilner, P., & Glick, I. (1998). Effects of psychoeducational intervention for married patients with bipolar disorder and their spouses. *Psychiatric Services, 49*, 531–533.

Goldstein, M. J., & Miklowitz, D. J. (1995). The effectiveness of psychoeducational family therapy in the treatment of schizophrenic disorders. *Journal of Martial and Family Therapy, 21*, 361–376.

Miklowitz, D. J., Axelson, D. A., Birmaher, B., George, E. L., Taylor, D. O., Schneck, C. D., . . . Brent, D. A. (2008). Family-focused treatment for adolescents with bipolar disorder: Results of a 2-year randomized trial. *Archive of General Psychiatry, 65*, 1053–1061.

Miklowitz, D. J., George, E. L., Richards, J. A., Simoneau, T. L., & Suddath, R. L. (2003). A randomized study of family-focused psychoeducation and pharmacotherapy in the outpatient management of bipolar disorder. *Archives of General Psychiatry, 60*, 904–912.

Miklowitz, D. J., Goldstein, M. J., & Nuechterlein, K. H. (1995). Verbal interactions in the families of schizophrenic and bipolar affective patients. *Journal of Abnormal Psychology, 104*, 268–276.

Miklowitz, D. J., Otto, M. W., Frank, E., Reilly-Harrington, N. A., Kogan, J. N., Sachs, G. S., . . . Wisniewski, S. R. (2007). Intensive psychosocial intervention enhances functioning in patients with bipolar depression: Results from a 9-month randomized controlled trial. *American Journal of Psychiatry, 164*, 1340–1347.

Miller, I., Solomon, D. A., Ryan, C. E., & Keitner, G. I. (2004). Does adjunctive family therapy enhance recovery from bipolar I mood episodes? *Journal of Affective Disorders, 82*, 431–436.

Rea, M. M., Tompson, M., Miklowitz, D. J., Goldstein, M. J., Hwang, S., & Mintz, J. (2003). Family focused treatment vs. individual treatment for bipolar disorder: Results of a randomized clinical trial. *Journal of Consulting and Clinical Psychology, 71*, 482–492.

Simoneau, T. L., Miklowitz, D. J., Richards, J. A., Saleem, R., & George, E. L. (1999). Bipolar disorder and family communication: Effects of a psychoeducational treatment program. *Journal of Abnormal Psychology, 108*, 588–597.

### Clinical Resources

Miklowitz, D. J., & Goldstein, M. J. (1997). *Bipolar disorder: A family-focused treatment approach*. New York, NY: Guilford Press.

### Training Opportunities

David J. Miklowitz, Department of Psychology, University of Colorado, Boulder, CO, miklow@psych.colorado.edu.

## For Interpersonal and Social Rhythm Therapy

### Empirical Support

Frank, E., Kupfer, D. J., Ehlers, C. L., Monk, T. H., Cornes, C., Carter, S., . . . Frankel, D. R. (1994). Interpersonal and social rhythm therapy for bipolar disorder: Integrating interpersonal and behavioral approaches. *The Behavior Therapist, 17*, 143–149.

Frank, E., Kupfer, D. J., Thase, M. E., Mallinger, A. G., Swartz, H. A., Fagiolini, A. M., . . . Monk, T. H. (2005). Two-year outcomes for interpersonal and social rhythm therapy in individuals with bipolar I disorder. *Archives of General Psychiatry, 62*, 996–1004.

Frank, E., Swartz, H. A., & Kupfer, D. J. (2000). Interpersonal and social rhythm therapy: Managing the chaos of bipolar disorder. *Biological Psychiatry, 48*, 593–604.

Miklowitz, D. J., Otto, M. W., Frank, E., Reilly-Harrington, N. A., Kogan, J. N., Sachs, G. S., . . . Wisniewski, S. R. (2007). Intensive psychosocial intervention enhances functioning in patients with bipolar depression: Results from a 9-month randomized controlled trial. *American Journal of Psychiatry, 164*, 1340–1347.

### Clinical Resources

Frank, E. (2005). *Treating bipolar disorder: A clinician's guide to interpersonal and social rhythm therapy*. New York, NY: Guilford Press.

Klerman, G. L., Weissman, M. M., & Rounsaville, B. J. (1995). *Interpersonal psychotherapy of depression*. New York, NY: Basic Books.

Monk, T. H., Kupfer, D. J., Frank, E., & Ritenour, A. M. (1991). The social rhythm metric (SRM): Measuring daily social rhythms over 12 weeks. *Psychiatry Research, 36*, 195–207.

Weissman, M. M., Markowitz, J., & Klerman, G. L. (2000). *Comprehensive guide to interpersonal psychotherapy*. New York, NY: Basic Books.

### Training Opportunities

Ellen Frank, Western Psychiatric Institute and Clinic, Pittsburgh, PA, FrankE@upmc.edu.

### Bibliotherapy Resources

Basco, M. R. (2005). *The bipolar workbook: Tools for controlling your mood swings*. New York, NY: Guilford Press.

Last, C. G. (2009). *When someone you love is bipolar: Help and support for you and your partner*. New York, NY: Guilford Press.

Miklowitz, D. J. (2010). *The bipolar disorder survival guide: What you and your family need to know* (2nd ed.). New York, NY: Guilford Press.

Owen, S., & Saunders, A. (2008). *Bipolar disorder: The ultimate guide*. Oxford, UK: Oneworld.

Note: Training opportunities information is from www.psychologicaltreatments.org.

CHAPTER 5

# How Do You Integrate Empirically Supported Treatments Into Treatment Planning?

This chapter is formatted differently from the others in this *Guide*. Rather than reviewing the *Chapter Review* questions and answers only, this chapter more closely follows the DVD and *Companion Workbook* to allow you to take participants through each step of the evidence-based treatment planning process.

This section of the DVD shows the viewer each step in the process of integrating ESTs into a treatment plan. It discusses each step of the treatment planning process for the identified problem (i.e., Behavioral Definitions, Goals, Objectives, and Treatment Interventions) and provides examples of how each can be written—with the objectives and interventions reflecting content consistent with the indicated EST. In this chapter, we have reproduced the examples of treatment plan statements shown on the DVD and included in the *Companion Workbook*. This gives you the option of stopping the DVD to discuss an example, or simply let it play.

For those interested in exploring issues related to the clinical delivery of the treatments discussed, vignettes are shown that demonstrate selected aspects of them. Each vignette is followed by a brief critique of the demonstration. The script of these vignettes, comments made in the critique, and a section allowing viewers to further critique are included in this *Guide* as well as the *Companion Workbook*. You can elect to facilitate this additional critique by viewers. Keep in mind that the vignettes demonstrate only selected aspects of the interventions discussed. They are informational in nature, to give the viewer an example of what a treatment might look like in its application, and are not intended to substitute for clinical training in the interventions discussed.

Following selected vignettes, references may be made to homework assignments that can be found and reprinted at www.wiley.com/go/bpdwb. These assignments also demonstrate selected therapeutic interventions consistent with those discussed in the DVD. These can also be reviewed and discussed at the facilitator's discretion.

Each section in this chapter is followed by section review questions, test-style questions, and an optional discussion question for use by the facilitator.

## Integrating ESTs into Treatment Planning

Construction of an empirically informed treatment plan for Bipolar Disorder involves integrating objectives and treatment interventions consistent with identified empirically supported treatments (ESTs) into a client's treatment plan after you have determined that the client's primary problem fits those described in the target population of the EST research. Of course, implementing ESTs must be done in consideration of important client, therapist, and therapeutic relationship factors—consistent with APA's definition of evidence-based practice.

## Definitions

The behavioral definition statements describe *how the problem manifests itself in the client*. Although there are several common features of bipolar disorder (BPD), the behavioral definition of BPD for your client will be unique and specific to him or her. Your assessment will need to identify which features best characterize your client's presentation. Accordingly, the *behavioral definition* section of the treatment plan is tailored to your individual client's clinical picture. After determining that BPD is the primary presenting problem, we then add to the treatment plan those behavioral manifestations of the disorder that define the client's unique expression of it.

Here is a list of behavioral definitions commonly used for BPD:

- Shows evidence of five (or more) major depressive episode symptoms (i.e., sadness, interest deficiency, guilt, energy loss, concentration deficits, appetite disturbance, psychomotor slowness, sleep disturbance, suicidal thoughts).
- Exhibits an abnormally and persistently elevated, expansive, or irritable mood with at least three manic symptoms (i.e., inflated self-esteem or grandiosity, decreased need for sleep, pressured speech, flight of ideas, distractibility, increased goal-directed activity or psychomotor agitation, excessive involvement in pleasurable, high-risk behavior).
- The elevated mood or irritability (mania) causes marked impairment in occupational functioning, social activities, or relationships with others, or necessitates hospitalization to prevent harm to self or others, or there are psychotic features.
- The elevated mood or irritability (hypomania) is not severe enough to cause marked impairment in social or occupational functioning, or to necessitate hospitalization, and there are no psychotic features, but the change is observable by others and is uncharacteristic of the person.

The first definition statement describes the classic symptoms of depression that can occur within BPD. The next statement describes symptoms of a manic episode.

The last two statements refer to the level of impairment that may result from these episodes. You may want to add behavioral definitions that best describe your particular client's clinical presentation.

# Goals

The next step in treatment planning is to determine long-term goals. Goals are broad statements describing what you and the client would like the result of therapy to be. One statement may suffice, but more than one can be used in the treatment plan. The following are examples of goals for the treatment of BPD:

- Normalize energy level and return to usual activities, good judgment, stable mood, more realistic expectations, and goal-directed behavior.
- Develop healthy cognitive patterns and beliefs about self and the world that lead to alleviation and help prevent the relapse of manic-depression symptoms.
- Alleviate depressed mood and return to previous level of effective functioning.
- Stabilize sleeping pattern, energy level, and appetite.
- Achieve a more reality-based orientation.
- Develop an increased understanding of bipolar disorder symptoms, as well as an understanding of the indicators of and the triggers for relapse.

You may want to develop other goals as well and add them to your plan.

# Objectives and Interventions

We now direct our attention to client objectives and therapist interventions consistent with research-supported treatments for BPD. Objectives are statements that describe *small, observable steps the client must achieve toward attaining the goal of successful treatment*. Intervention statements describe the *actions taken by the therapist to assist the client in achieving his/her objectives*. Each objective must be paired with at least one intervention. We begin with objectives and interventions related to assessment.

### Assessment

As with all treatment, a thorough assessment is important to developing an optimal treatment plan. The assessment phase of treatment typically involves obtaining a detailed description of the nature and history of the symptoms, as well as the impact on the client's social, occupational, and interpersonal functioning.

Psychological tests or objective measures may be used to supplement the clinical interview and/or track treatment response. Because the effects of BPD can be very severe, an assessment of the client's need for a protective environment, such as a psychiatric hospital or a residential crisis unit, should be performed. Because psychological treatments for BPD are adjuncts to medication treatment, a psychiatric evaluation is a necessary consideration in the plan.

Table 5.1 contains examples of assessment objectives and interventions for bipolar disorder.

## Table 5.1 Assessment Objectives and Interventions

| Objectives | Interventions |
| --- | --- |
| 1. Describe mood state, energy level, amount of control over thoughts, and sleeping pattern. | 1. Assess the client for classic signs of elevated, expansive, or irritable mood: pressured speech, high-risk behavior, euphoria, flight of ideas, reduced need for sleep, inflated self-esteem, high energy, etc.<br>2. Assess the client's level of elation: hypomanic, manic, or psychotic and the degree of impact on the client's social, occupational, and interpersonal functioning.<br>3. Assess the client for signs of depression and whether there is evidence of cycling from depression to mania or hypomania. |
| 2. Complete psychological testing or objective questionnaires for assessing mania/hypomania. | 1. Administer to the client psychological instruments designed to objectively assess mania/hypomania (e.g., Minnesota Multiphasic Personality Inventory-2 [MMPI-2], Personality Assessment Inventory [PAI] by Morey); give the client feedback regarding the results of the assessment. |
| 3. Complete psychological testing to assess communication patterns within the family or with significant others. | 1. Arrange for the administration of an objective assessment instrument for evaluating communication patterns with family/significant others, particularly expressed emotion (e.g., Perceived Criticism Scale by Hooley and Teasdale); evaluate results and process feedback with the client and family. |
| 4. Agree to placement in an environment that ensures safety to self and others. | 1. Perform an assessment of the client's ability to remain safe in the community, including level of manic behavior, impulsivity, natural and programmatic supports, and access to potentially unsafe situations.<br>2. Arrange for admission into a crisis residential unit or psychiatric hospital if the client is judged to be at imminent risk of harm to him/herself or to others. |
| 5. Cooperate with psychiatric evaluation as to the need for medication and/or hospitalization to stabilize mood and energy. | 1. Arrange for a psychiatric evaluation of the client for pharmacotherapy (e.g., Lithium carbonate, Depakote, Lamictil, etc.).<br>2. Monitor the client's reaction to the psychotropic medication (e.g., compliance, side effects, and effectiveness) and report reactions to the prescribing physician.<br>3. Monitor the client's symptom improvement toward stabilization sufficient to allow participation in psychotherapy. |

## Psychoeducation

A typical feature of many ESTs for BPD is initial and ongoing psychoeducation. Common emphases include helping the client learn about the disorder, the treatment, and its rationale. Psychoeducation for bipolar disorder may involve individual or group sessions. The tendency for the illness to relapse and the need for medication compliance are common emphases. The role of stress and an unregulated lifestyle as triggers for relapse are underscored as well, as are ways to manage these triggers to minimize the risk of relapse. Readings or other educational material may be recommended to supplement psychoeducation done in session. In addition to the content conveyed in psychoeducation, it is important to instill hope in clients and have them on board as a partner in the treatment process. With ESTs, discussing their demonstrated efficacy with clients may also be useful.

Examples of an objective and interventions consistent with these psychoeducational emphases appear in number 6 and its associated interventions, as seen in Table 5.2.

In addition to being a common component of ESTs for BPD, psychoeducation, in particular group psychoeducation, is also a stand-alone empirically supported treatment program. Should the client decide to enroll in such a program, that objective and its associated intervention can be described, as seen in objective number seven of Table 5.2.

---

**Key Points**

COMMON EMPHASES OF INITIAL PSYCHOEDUCATION INCLUDE:
1. Teaching the client about the nature and etiology of the diagnosed condition.
2. Informing the client regarding the various treatment options consistent with the best available evidence.
3. Explaining the treatment and its rationale.
4. Utilizing reading or other educational assignments as homework, if needed, to facilitate an understanding of the psychoeducational goals.

---

Psychoeducation, particularly group psychoeducation, is also a stand-alone, empirically supported treatment program for bipolar disorder.

Table 5.2 contains examples of psychoeducational objectives and interventions for Bipolar Disorder.

## Table 5.2   Psychoeducation Objectives and Interventions

| Objectives | Interventions |
| --- | --- |
| 6. Verbalize an understanding of the causes for, symptoms of, and treatment of manic, hypomanic, mixed, and/or depressive episodes. | 1. Teach the client, family, and relevant others, using all modalities necessary, about the signs, symptoms, and phasic relapsing nature of the client's mood episodes; destigmatize and normalize.<br>2. Teach the client a stress diathesis model of bipolar disorder that emphasizes the strong role of a biological predisposition to mood episodes that is vulnerable to stresses that are manageable and the need for medication compliance (or assign "Why I Dislike Taking My Medication" in the *Adult Psychotherapy Homework Planner*, 2nd ed., by Jongsma).<br>3. Provide the client with a rationale for treatment involving ongoing medication and psychosocial treatment to recognize, manage, and reduce biological and psychological vulnerabilities that could precipitate relapse. |
| 7. Attend a group psychoeducational program designed to inform members as to the nature of and causes for bipolar disorder as well as emphasize the need to comply with medication and other treatment and ways to minimize relapse. | 1. Conduct a series of 21 group sessions that teach clients the psychological, biological, and social influences in the development of BPD, its biological and psychological treatment, illness management skills (e.g., early warning signs, common triggers, coping strategies), problem solving focused on life goals, and a personal care plan that emphasizes a regular sleep routine and stress regulation (see the Life Goals Program by Bauer and McBride). |

## Demonstration Vignette
### *Group Psychoeducation for Bipolar Disorder*

Here we present the transcript of the dialogue depicted in the Group Psychoeducation therapy vignette.

| | |
|---|---|
| Therapist: | Welcome, everyone, to our third meeting. I'd like to begin today with a brief summary of our first two sessions. We began by describing the purpose of the program as teaching what a bipolar disorder is and how to best cope with it. We explained the rules of the group, including rules regarding mutual respect for each other, confidentiality, attendance, punctuality, and level of participation. Then each of us told everyone our name and gave a little information about ourselves. But then, as you may remember, we had a little fun together and went around the group again saying our name and trying to say the names of every person before us. [group laughter] Poor Jack was the last one, which meant that he had to remember everyone else's name. Have you recovered from that stress yet, Jack? |
| Jack: | Just barely. (group laughter) It only took me *three* go-arounds until I got everyone's name right. |
| Therapist: | You were a good sport about it, Jack. Thank you. In our second session we discussed that bipolar disorder is an illness in which the mood is not always stable. We compared it to having a "faulty thermostat" in the brain that results in moods changing, sometimes quickly, and often not related to what is going on around the person. Moods can go from being elated with uncontrolled energy to feeling depression and not interested in anything—sometimes without any reasonable, external cause. We asked you to share what moods have been like for each of you. We heard that some of you have more episodes of depression with only brief swings into mild manic states, while others have more severe episodes of mania. The patterns varied from one individual to another. |
| | Well, today I'd like to talk more about what causes bipolar illness and start with what you've found that triggers your mood episodes. Who can share with us what they think has triggered a shift in their mood in the past? (pause) |
| Client A: | I found if my wife works too much overtime, I can get real frustrated and then depressed. |
| Therapist: | Okay, thank you, [insert a name]. So in this instance, a relationship stress triggered a depression swing. Someone else? |
| Jack: | Sometimes, even if I'm tired, I think I don't need more than an hour or two of sleep to keep me going, and then I stay awake, and then I'm off to the races. |
| Therapist: | Okay. So you've noticed, Jack, that a manic swing can begin when you break your routine and don't get proper sleep? |
| Jack: | Yeah. |
| Therapist: | I want to point out, using these two examples, a fairly common misunderstanding about mood swings. Bipolar swings in mood are not *caused* by these types of environmental events, but they may be *triggered* by them. The real cause of Jack's mood shift, for example, even though it's triggered by breaking from his usual work/sleep routine, is actually *internal* and *biochemical*. The causes of these mood changes are based in these biochemical mechanisms in the brain. Jack, and the rest of you as well, were born with this "faulty thermostat" in your brain. Inherited genetic makeup is the cause of the inability to regulate the mood. There's strong evidence for an inherited tendency, called a predisposition, to develop bipolar disorder in most patients. Nearly two-thirds of people with bipolar disorder have one or more family members who have struggled with a mood disorder of some kind. |

*(continued)*

> Why is it important for the patient and family to know that bipolar disorder is caused by genetics and brain chemistry?
>
> Client B: Well, it helps because it means we don't need to blame *ourselves* for it.
>
> Client C: Yeah, and maybe our *families* can know that it's not our fault. We can't control it like they can.
>
> Jack: Does this mean there's nothing we can do to help ourselves?
>
> Therapist: Good question, Jack. Patients are not to blame for this illness any more than a person with diabetes is to blame for it. But, like someone with diabetes, the person with bipolar disorder needs to accept that medication is necessary to help regulate the biochemical side of this disorder and take his/her medication consistently. And just like those with diabetes are disciplined about their diets, the person with bipolar disorder needs to be careful about maintaining regular sleep and a low-stress routine. You can help moderate this disorder by making some lifestyle changes that reduce the events that can trigger an episode. Maintaining a regular routine and getting proper rest is one of the ways to control episode triggers, but these lifestyle changes are not enough to treat this illness. Medication is *crucial* to stabilizing the brain chemistry.
>
> Let's talk a little about our views of medication and its role in managing this disorder.

## Critique of the Psychoeducation Demonstration Vignette

### The following points were made in the critique:

a. Session began with a good summary of previous group meetings.
b. Therapist drew examples of triggers from the clients.
c. Important distinction was made between triggers and causes.
d. Critical emphasis was placed on the need for medication compliance because of the underlying biological cause for BPD.
e. The concept of the need for regulating lifestyle is introduced.
f. The therapist is setting the groundwork for each client having a personal care plan.
g. This psychoeducation work can be done effectively in one-to-one sessions as well as in groups.

### Additional points that could be made:

a. The therapist could have drawn more content from the client group before providing factual information.
b. Therapist made good use of a social ice-breaker of the "name game" in the first session.

**Comments you would like to make:**

_____
_____
_____
_____

**Homework:** The homework exercise listed in the psychoeducation intervention (see Table 5.2), "Why I Dislike Taking My Medication," allows the client to express his/her negative reaction to mood-stabilizing medication, but it also helps him or her identify the advantages of taking the medication consistently and responsibly. The exercise "Sleep Pattern Record" teaches sleep induction methods as well as allowing the client to record his/her sleep pattern for the week (*Adult Psychotherapy Homework Planner*, 2nd ed., by Jongsma). To help the client identify warning signs related to thinking, emotions, and behavior that may be related to a manic episode, assign "Early Warning Signs of Mania/Hypomania." The exercise "Planning for Stability" is designed to help the client think through the issues related to establishing a consistent and healthy routine, including daily schedule, medication management, diet, sleep hygiene, pleasurable activities, and so forth (*Addiction Treatment Homework Planner*, 4th ed., by Finley and Lenz). (See www.wiley.com/go/bpdwb)

## Assessment/Psychoeducation Review

1. What are some common general emphases of psychoeducation?

---

COMMON GENERAL EMPHASES OF INITIAL PSYCHOEDUCATION INCLUDE:

- Teaching the client about the nature and etiology of the diagnosed condition
- Informing the client regarding the various treatment options consistent with the best available evidence
- Explaining the treatment and its rationale
- Utilizing reading or other educational assignments as homework, if needed, to facilitate an understanding of psychoeducational goals
- Instilling hope
- Building rapport and a therapeutic alliance

---

2. What are some psychoeducational emphases particular to bipolar disorder?

- The relapsing nature of the disorder
- The need for medication and compliance with it
- The role of stress and an unregulated lifestyle as triggers for relapse
- How managing triggers helps minimize the risk of relapse
- Others can be elaborated at the facilitator's discretion

## Talking Points

Compliance with medication is a common theme of psychoeducation for bipolar disorder. Consider facilitating a discussion of likely reasons for noncompliance and strategies for increasing adherence. This could be a wide-ranging discussion. Examples to get it started are as follows:

REASONS FOR NONCOMPLIANCE:
- Lack of knowledge about the disorder
- Lack of knowledge about the role of medication
- Lack of belief in the need for medication or its effectiveness
- Lack of insight into having the disorder
- Lack of motivation
- Preference for the euphoric mood
- Fear of side effects
- Practical issues in taking the medication reliably

STRATEGIES TO IMPROVE COMPLIANCE:
- Filling knowledge gaps
- Improving insight by looking at the evidence of the disorder in the client's life
- Enlisting support from social systems
- Building a therapeutic alliance where medication adherence is one of the objectives
- Explaining the rationale for medication
- Addressing fears through cognitive restructuring
- Assessing for obstacles to compliance and problem-solving them
- Doing motivational interventions

## Assessment/Psychoeducation Review Test Question

1. Although psychoeducation permeates most research-supported treatments for bipolar disorder, which of the following forms of it is a well-established psychological treatment for bipolar mania, according to Division 12 of the APA?

    A. Cognitive-behavioral therapy (CBT)
    B. Family-focused therapy (FFT)
    C. Group psychoeducation (GP)
    D. Individual psychoeducation (IP)
    Answer: C

## Cognitive-Behavioral Therapy

The objective and therapeutic interventions descriptive of cognitive behavior therapy (CBT) for BPD highlight the major features of the treatment. The interventions describe psychoeducation related to the illness's biological roots and the associated need for medication compliance, exploring depressive or manic self-talk and beliefs, identifying and challenging biases, generating alternatives, and prediction testing through use of behavioral experiments. Homework assignments related to any of these tasks are used commonly in the therapy. In some CBT approaches to BPD, an emphasis is placed on the acquisition of cognitive-behavioral coping and relapse prevention skills, such as maintaining a regular sleep/wake cycle and avoiding or managing triggers of mood episodes.

---

**Key Points**

COMPONENTS OF CBT FOR MANIA
- Psychoeducation
- Cognitive restructuring
- Lifestyle/activity stabilization
- Regulating sleep patterns
- Various behavioral techniques (e.g., skills training, stimulus control)

---

Table 5.3 contains examples of a CBT objective and interventions for BPD.

**Table 5.3  Cognitive-Behavioral Therapy Objective and Interventions**

| Objective | Interventions |
|---|---|
| 8. Identify and replace thoughts and behaviors that trigger manic or depressive symptoms. | 1. Reinforce to the client the psychoeducational content that bipolar illness is biologically based, the need for medication compliance, and heeding the early warning signs of an episode that needs professional intervention.<br>2. Using cognitive therapy techniques, explore the client's biased schema and self-talk that mediate his/her elevated or depressive mood; assist him/her in generating thoughts that correct for the biases; use behavioral experiments to test fearful versus alternative predictions (see Cognitive *Therapy for Bipolar Disorder: A Therapist's Guide to Concepts, Methods, and Practice* by Lam, Jones, Hayward, and Bright).<br>3. Assign the client a homework exercise in which he or she identifies fearful or expansive self-talk, identifies biases in the self-talk, generates alternatives, and tests though behavioral experiments; review and reinforce success, providing corrective feedback toward improvement.<br>3. Teach the client cognitive-behavioral coping and relapse prevention skills, including delaying impulsive actions, structured scheduling of daily activities, keeping a regular sleep routine, avoiding unrealistic goal striving, using relaxation procedures, identifying and avoiding episode triggers such as stimulant drug use, alcohol consumption, breaking sleep routine, or exposing self to high stress (see *Cognitive Therapy for Bipolar Disorder* by Lam, Jones, Hayward, and Bright). |

# Demonstration Vignette
## *Cognitive Behavioral Therapy*

Here we present the transcript of the dialogue depicted in the Cognitive-Behavioral Therapy vignette.

| | |
|---|---|
| Therapist: | Jack, I can see on your mood and activity schedule that you had an up-and-down week. You cut back on your overtime and did a few more things with the family earlier this week. |
| Client: | Yeah, I told Carol that if I'm not home by 5:30 to call me. She had to call a few times at the beginning of the week, but then I remembered and got myself home. |
| Therapist: | Good. And you spent more time with your family doing some nice things on those evenings? |
| Client: | Yeah, we did some relaxing things. We cooked together, watched some movies, played some games. It was good. |
| Therapist: | Your sleep was good those nights, too—7 hours. And did you notice how your mood ratings those days were good, too—calm at a 6 or 7? |
| Client: | Yeah, I was feeling pretty good until Thursday. I don't know. I just woke up feeling stressed and tired. I was wired all day, but exhausted at the same time. |
| Therapist: | It looks like you went to bed very late Wednesday night. |
| Client: | I did. I watched a movie after everyone went to bed. |
| Therapist: | Then it looks like you had a tense day Thursday, took a nap when you got home, stayed up Thursday night, and felt the same way Friday as you did Thursday. This is a change from the schedule you've been on. |
| Client: | Yeah, I just got tired and had to nap, and then I wasn't sleepy Friday night. But then Carol reminded me about the sleep hygiene stuff we talked about. So I didn't nap Friday, went to bed with her, and woke up at my regular time. Same thing on Saturday and it helped. |
| Therapist: | And your mood during the weekend was better? |
| Client: | Yeah, it was. I just screwed up my sleeping pattern and it threw me off. |
| Therapist: | It started when you decided to watch that late movie on Wednesday. What made you decide to stay up? |
| Client: | I don't know. I just had such a good time watching a movie with Carol and the kids, and I guess I just wanted it to keep going, you know? |
| Therapist: | Keep what going? |
| Client: | The good feeling. I mean even though the kids went to bed, I was feeling pretty good and just wanted to stay up and enjoy it. |
| Therapist: | I see. So, in terms of your self-talk, what do you think you were saying to yourself at that exact moment? |
| Client: | I think I was just saying something like, "You feel good! Let's keep this going." |
| Therapist: | Okay. So the idea was that staying up would make the feeling last, and you wanted the feeling to last. |
| Client: | Yeah, I suppose. |
| Therapist: | Did you know you might pay for it the next day? |
| Client: | Yeah, kinda. I guess I just forgot. |
| Therapist: | Forgot what? |
| Client: | Forgot to, you know [says somewhat dramatically], listen to the voice of reason. |
| Therapist: | [smiles] That darned voiced of reason. Did you forget it or ignore it? |
| Client: | Yeah, I heard it. I just ignored it. |

*(continued)*

| | |
|---|---|
| Therapist: | Was the "feel-good" voice right—you had a good time after that? |
| Client: | Actually, no. It wasn't the same without Carol and the kids. I just kind of vegged out, and before I knew it, it was late. |
| Therapist: | And the next few days weren't so hot either? |
| Client: | No. |
| Therapist: | So, going with what the feeling was at the moment, and ignoring your other voice didn't pay off so well? |
| Client: | No, not so much. |
| Therapist: | So, Jack, can we use this experience to help you at those moments when you face this decision? |
| Client: | I think if I can just remember how I felt later it might help me. |
| Therapist: | How can we do that—help you remember that a regular sleep pattern is very important in regulating your mood? |
| Client: | I don't know. |
| Therapist: | Why don't we talk about ways to strengthen that decision-making skill? |
| Client: | Yeah, I think I'm going to need to. |

## Critique of the Cognitive-Behavioral Therapy Demonstration Vignette

**The following points were made in the critique:**

   a. The important role of homework is underlined.
   b. The client's sleep pattern is reviewed as one of the triggers for mood change. The therapist highlights how a change in activity level can trigger a change in mood, supporting the rationale for activity regulation.
   c. The therapist increases the client's awareness of his self-talk.
   d. The therapist turns the client's attention to the fact that when he did not listen to the "voice of reason," the result was not as he expected or wished for.

**Additional point that could be made:**

   a. Therapist could have been more direct in describing the "prediction testing" that was behind her inquiry about the result of his listening to his unhealthy self-talk—in essence empowering the client with a better understanding of the process.

**Comments you would like to make:**

_____
_____
_____
_____

**Homework:** The homework "Why I Dislike Taking My Medication" allows the client to express his/her negative reaction to mood-stabilizing medication, but it also helps him or her identify the advantages of taking the medication consistently and responsibly. The exercise "Sleep Pattern Record" teaches sleep induction methods as well as allowing the client to record his/her sleep pattern for the week. Cognitive therapy principles are taught through the exercise "Negative Thoughts Trigger Negative Feelings." The client reads about and identifies common types of distorted thinking and then must generate positive, more realistic thoughts to replace his/her dysfunctional thoughts.

To lead the client to use problem-solving techniques rather than impulsive action, the exercise "Plan Before Acting" could be assigned (*Adult Psychotherapy Homework Planner*, 2nd ed., by Jongsma). Finally, the homework exercise "Coping with Addiction and Mood Disorders or Bereavement" guides clients to an awareness of the destructive role of self-medication using alcohol or other illicit drugs for emotional distress and to explore healthy alternative ways to cope. (See www.wiley.com/go/bpdwb)

## Cognitive-Behavioral Therapy Review

1. What are the key components of CBT for BPD?

> CBT interventions include psychoeducation related to the illness's biological roots and the associated need for medication compliance, exploring depressive or manic self-talk and beliefs, identifying and challenging biases, generating alternatives, and prediction testing through use of behavioral experiments. Homework assignments related to any of these tasks are used commonly in the therapy. In some CBT approaches to bipolar disorder, an emphasis is placed on the acquisition of cognitive-behavioral coping and relapse prevention skills, such as maintaining a regular sleep/wake cycle and avoiding or managing triggers of mood episodes.
>
> KEY COMPONENTS OF CBT FOR MANIA
> - Psychoeducation
> - Cognitive restructuring
> - Lifestyle/activity stabilization
> - Regulating sleep patterns
> - Various behavioral techniques (e.g., skills training, stimulus control)

> **Talking Points**
>
> A staple of CBT for BPD is teaching patients how to identify and respond to prodromes (early signs and symptoms) of mood episodes. Consider facilitating a discussion about common prodromes of manic/hypomanic and/or depressive episodes. You might ask, "What might be some common early warning signs that a patient may be slipping into a [type of episode]?".
>
> CONSIDERATIONS:
> - Changes in mood, cognition, or behavior, including changes in sleep, are common domains for prodromes.
> - Changes in interpersonal behavior (e.g., withdrawal, irritations, conflicts) may also serve as warning signs that mood and/or cognition is changing.
> - Feedback from family or friends may also signal prodromes.
> - You may want to make the point that in therapy these signs would be explored on a client-to-client basis, often by reviewing past episodes with the stable client as well as with their significant others.

## Cognitive-Behavioral Therapy Review Test Question

1. True or False: Cognitive therapy grew out of its use with unipolar depression. In its application to mania, it also targets the overly positive and grandiose thoughts characteristic of manic episodes.
   Answer: True

## Family-Focused Therapy

In general, family-focused therapy (FFT) emphasizes psychoeducation related to BPD as well as personal and interpersonal skills training that are relapse preventative. As seen in Table 5.4, the approach begins with family sessions that use psychoeducation to help the family understand the rationale for the therapy. The next intervention statement describes the use of role-play, modeling, and feedback to teach active listening, effective communication, and problem-solving skills that minimize expressed emotion in the family and help regulate the patient's emotions, enhance interpersonal communication, and resolve problems effectively. Intervention statement number three describes the use of homework to facilitate the learning process around healthy communication skills in the client's family.

## Key Points

MAJOR EMPHASES OF FAMILY-FOCUSED THERAPY (FFT)
- Psychoeducation
- Communication enhancement training
- Problem-solving skills training
- FFT emphasizes strategies that help patients regulate their emotions, enhance interpersonal communication, and resolve problems effectively.

Table 5.4 contains examples of a Family-Focused Therapy objective and interventions for Bipolar Disorder.

### Table 5.4  Family-Focused Therapy Objective and Interventions

| Objective | Interventions |
| --- | --- |
| 9. Family members learn about bipolar disorder, factors that influence it, and the role of medication and therapy, while learning skills that help manage it and improve the quality of life of the family and its members. | 1. Conduct psychoeducation with family members, emphasizing the biological nature of bipolar disorder, the need for medication and medication adherence, risk factors for relapse such as personal and interpersonal triggers, and the importance of communication, problem solving, and early episode intervention.<br>2. Using structured exercises, teach the family that strong negative expressed emotion (e.g., hostility, pity, criticism) can trigger relapse of bipolar episodes; use role-play, modeling, and feedback to teach respectful, reflective, attentive, active listening and problem-solving skills (see *Bipolar Disorder: A Family-Focused Approach* by Miklowitz and Goldstein).<br>3. Assign the client and family homework exercises to use and record use of newly learned communication enhancement therapy skills; process the results in session. |

## Demonstration Vignette
### *Family-Focused Therapy*

Here we present the transcript of the dialogue depicted in the Family-Focused Therapy vignette.

Therapist: In our last session we talked about improving communication in the family by using active listening. I gave you a handout to read more about it at home. We discussed the four key elements of active listening that we summarized in the acronym ROAR: "R" is for Reflect—or summarize or paraphrase what you heard the speaker say; "O" is for Opinion—that's hold back on expressing your judgment or opinion until the speaker is finished; do not interrupt to disagree; "A" is for Attentiveness—keep good eye contact with the speaker and use body language or gestures or encouraging comments like "Uh-huh," "Okay," "Go on"; and the last "R" is for Respect—be honest but respectful in your response to what the speaker said.

Does this sound familiar to all of you?

Jack: Yeah.

Wife (Carol): Yes, it does.

Daughter (Danielle): Yep.

Carol: I tried it out even though you said we would be practicing it today.

Therapist: Okay, very good. How did it go for you?

Carol: It was hard for me to be patient and hold off on expressing my opinion or judgment until Jack was finished saying what he wanted to say. I got too defensive, I guess. I started attacking him, and I know that wasn't good. When he's depressed, it's hard for me to remember that this is the illness talking and he can't control these mood swings.

Danielle: That's my problem, too. I get frustrated with him being down for no reason, but I'm learning more about bipolar being caused by changes in his brain that he inherited. It does make me a little more patient now.

Therapist: Good insights from both of you. Jack, you want to comment on this?

Jack: I knew Carol was trying to use active listening when I complained about not being able to bring enough money home for us. I get like that when I'm depressed. I feel a little brighter today.

| | |
|---|---|
| Therapist: | Okay, I hear that you blame yourself for the family's financial situation, and you make it worse than it is when you're in a depressed mood. |
| Jack: | That's right. |
| Therapist: | I'd like to just role-play this little scenario between you and Carol with Danielle and I watching and listening. Are you both willing to try this? |
| Jack: | Okay. |
| Carol: | I'll try to do it better this time. |
| Therapist: | Perfect. Jack, why don't you start by complaining. Carol, you try to use the ROAR techniques. |
| Jack: | Okay. Well, I just said something like, "I'm tired of us being broke all the time and not able to make enough for us to get ahead. I've never gotten the promotions or the raises we need." |
| Carol: | Uh-huh. (Nods and looks Jack in the eye.) |
| Jack: | I'm afraid you're just going to dump me and find someone else who can provide better for you and Danielle. |
| Carol: | I hear you blaming yourself, Jack, and thinking I'm unhappy with you. So unhappy, that you believe I'm thinking about getting a divorce. But, Jack, I know you work hard and do your best. This is your depression talking. I'm not unhappy with you, and I'm not going anywhere. |
| Therapist: | That was excellent, Carol. You were very attentive. You reflected what you heard. You didn't interrupt or lash out with an angry opinion. You were respectful in your response. Excellent. What did you think, Danielle? |
| Danielle: | That was good. I'm not sure I can do that, but I know I have to be more patient with Dad. |
| Therapist: | Okay. Well, let's work with this some more and talk about how we can implement active listening at home this week. I'd also like each of you to bring a journal entry next week that summarizes an instance of active listening that you were a part of. |

### Critique of the Family-Focused Therapy Demonstration Vignette

**The following points were made in the critique:**

a. Session focuses on communication enhancement training using the acronym ROAR for aspects of active listening to help the family remember the four points.

b. The psychoeducation is resulting in the family members showing a gain in insight into the biological basis for Bipolar Disorder.

c. Role-play is used to train the family in the active listening ROAR technique.

d. The therapist highlights and reinforces the wife's successful use of active listening.

e. Homework is assigned to consolidate the gains in implementing healthy communication through active listening.

### Additional points that could be made:

a. Both the wife and daughter verbalized an awareness of their own communication failures. Reinforce this insight.
b. The therapist did a nice job of bringing in the daughter by asking for her feedback on her mother's role-play.
c. Use of the ROAR acronym is one of many technical options for teaching communication skills. Therapists should strive to have a variety of options to allow for flexibility and facilitate adaptability to any particular client or family.

**Comments you would like to make:**

_____
_____
_____
_____

**Homework:** To help family members and the client express their thoughts and feelings regarding the client's inconsistent use of critical mood-stabilizing medication, the exercise "My Mom Just Won't Stay On Her Medication" can be assigned (*Family Therapy Homework Planner*, 2nd ed., by Bevilacqua and Dattilio). "Early Warning Signs of Mania/Hypomania" (*Addiction Treatment Homework Planner*, 4th ed., by Finley and Lenz) can help the client identify thinking, emotions, and behaviors that may be related to triggering a full manic episode. The family could work on this assignment together, because they may see signs that the client is not aware of. Problem-solving skills can be taught to the family through the use of "Applying Problem-Solving to Interpersonal Conflict" (*Adult Psychotherapy Homework Planner*, 2nd ed., by Jongsma). (See www.wiley.com/go/bpdwb)

## Family-Focused Therapy Review

1. What are the major emphases of FFT?

---

**MAJOR EMPHASES OF FAMILY-FOCUSED THERAPY (FFT)**
- Psychoeducation
- Communication enhancement training
- Problem-solving skills training
- FFT emphasizes strategies that help patients regulate their emotions, enhance interpersonal communication, and resolve problems effectively.

---

## Interpersonal and Social Rhythm Therapy

> **Talking Points**
>
> As noted, FFT emphasizes strategies that help patients regulate their emotions, enhance interpersonal communication, and resolve problems effectively. Consider facilitating a discussion about how this approach might work to help prevent relapse or recurrence (i.e., the return of an episode after a period of recovery) of mood episodes. You might ask, "In your opinion, how would doing psychoeducation, enhancing communication skills, and teaching problem solving work to help prevent relapse or recurrence of mood episodes?"
>
> Answers to this question will reflect how participants conceptualize mechanisms of therapeutic action. Examples include the following:
>
> - Psychoeducation may enhance medication adherence, may increase insight and acceptance of the disorder that could improve compliance, and/or reduced self- and other blaming of the patient, thus reducing conflict that could lead to patient decompensation.
> - These interventions may help patients and families recognize and manage prodromes (early warning signs) of relapse or recurrence that might help prevent patient decompensation.
> - Skills training may reduce interpersonal conflict, expressed emotion, and stress on the patient and family that otherwise could lead to patient decompensation.
> - Interventions may increase social support of the patient that would serve as a relapse preventative strength.
> - Others

## Family-Focused Therapy Review Test Question

1. Which of the following are the core interventions of family-focused therapy (FFT)?
   a. Psychoeducation about the biological basis of bipolar disorder and the need for medication adherence.
   b. Communication skills training that minimizes negative expressed emotion.
   c. Problem-solving skills training to reduce the risk that problems may lead to a relapse of mood episodes.
   d. Psychoeducation, communication enhancement training, and problem-solving skills training.

   Answer: D

## Interpersonal and Social Rhythm Therapy

Our final set of objectives and interventions reflects interpersonal and social rhythm therapy (IPSRT). As seen in Table 5.5, objectives 10 and 11 summarize the client's essential tasks within this treatment approach. The first describes establishing and maintaining a regular pattern of daily activities, such as mealtimes, hours of sleep, and social and work activities (i.e, the client's social rhythm). The therapist and client assess the client's daily routine and work to develop a predictable rhythm of balanced activities that are rewarding and not over- or understimulating.

Additionally, this therapy calls for the therapist to engage the client in a process of conflict resolution related to interpersonal relationships through the use of interpersonal therapy. The Interpersonal Inventory is conducted to assess, in part, current and past issues related to grief, role disputes, role transitions, and interpersonal skills deficits. The next intervention describes the use of client-centered techniques that characterize the therapy. They also summarize this therapy's use of a "rescue protocol" to restore medication compliance, an adequate sleep routine, and low-stress relationships.

---

### Key Points

- IPSRT aims to establish an optimal social rhythm, referring to a rewarding and consistent balance of activity including the sleep/wake cycle.
- It also uses interpersonal therapy techniques to help clients identify and resolve interpersonal problems that may make them vulnerable to future mood episodes.

---

Table 5.5 contains examples of Interpersonal and Social Rhythm Therapy objectives and interventions for Bipolar Disorder.

### Table 5.5  Interpersonal and Social Rhythm Therapy Objectives and Interventions

| Objective | Interventions |
|---|---|
| 10. Maintain a pattern of regular rhythm in daily activities. | 1. Explore and assess the client's daily activities using interview and the Social Rhythm Metric.<br>2. Assist the client in establishing a more routine pattern of daily activities, such as sleeping, eating, solitary and social activities, and exercise; use and review a form to schedule, assess, and modify these activities so that they occur in a predictable rhythm every day.<br>3. Engage the client in a balanced schedule of "behavioral activation" by gradually increasing activities that have a high likelihood for pleasure and mastery (see "Identify and Schedule Pleasant Activities" in *Adult Psychotherapy Homework Planner*, 2nd ed., by Jongsma); use activity and mood monitoring to facilitate an optimal balance of activity; reinforce success. |

# Interpersonal and Social Rhythm Therapy 45

| Objective | Interventions |
|---|---|
| 11. Discuss and resolve troubling personal and interpersonal issues. | 1. Use the semistructured Interpersonal Inventory to assess the client's current and past significant relationships for grief, interpersonal role disputes, interpersonal role transitions, and interpersonal skills deficits.<br>2. Use interpersonal therapy techniques to explore and resolve issues surrounding grief, role disputes, role transitions, and social skills deficits; provide support and strategies for resolving any issues of conflict.<br>3. Establish a "rescue protocol" with the client and significant others to manage clinical deterioration; include medication use, sleep restoration, and conflict-free social support. |

## Demonstration Vignette

### Interpersonal and Social Rhythm Therapy

Here we present the transcript of the dialogue depicted in the Interpersonal and Social Rhythm Therapy vignette.

Therapist: [showing form to patient] Okay, Jack, here's that form we're going to use to get a sense of your social rhythm, like we talked about.

Client: Okay. How do I use this? These things can be confusing, you know?

Therapist: Yes, they can; let's take a look at it. Right here is the list of activities that we want to record. As you can see, for each day, you record what time you got out of bed, what time you had your first contact with a person, what time you began your work, what time you ate dinner, and what time you went to bed.

Client: It just follows my day.... You know, I don't always do those things the same time every day. It may be different day-to-day.

Therapist: Oh sure, I understand. That's what we want to see—when you're actually doing these things.

*(continued)*

Client: Okay, but we're also trying to get these things on more of a schedule, right? [Therapist nods.] You still want me to try to do that, too?

Therapist: Yes, that's what this is right here [points to the form]. It's called the "target time." We'll put the time we're shooting for there, and here's where we record what time each of these things actually happens that day.

Client: I see. What if I don't make the target time?

Therapist: Well, here's the plan: First we'll fill in the target times together, and then you just record the actual times during the week and bring the form back. We'll take a look at it each week. If we see that the actual time is different than the target, then we'll look at possible reasons why and see if there are ways to get closer to the target time. In other words, we'll problem-solve. Sound okay?

Client: Yeah, things are better at home.

Therapist: How so?

Client: Everybody's just a lot more respectful of each other, you know?

Therapist: So Carol and the kids are more respectful of you? How so?

Client: They don't just write me off right away, like if I don't make complete sense to them the first time, especially the kids.

Therapist: Okay, and you're more respectful of them?

Client: Yeah, I don't get quite as frustrated thinking they're blowing me off or something—like we were talking about.

Therapist: You don't jump to a bad conclusion as much?

Client: No, I just try to take it for what it is, instead of spinning it.

Therapist: And that's helped?

Client: Yeah, 'cause most of the time they're just asking. They aren't trying to judge me or anything. I'm just trying to take it for what it is.

Therapist: So these things have been frustrating you with your supervisor?

Client: Yeah. I mean, he knows what I do. Why would he have to ask unless he thinks I'm not doing them?

Therapist: So when he asked about whether you got the machine cleaned, you thought he was criticizing you.

Client: [pauses] Yeah.

[Client and therapist pause]

Client: You think I'm reading into it with him?

Therapist: I don't know, Jack, perhaps. Did you just take his question for what it was, like with Carol and taking the trash out, or did you add a spin to it?

Client: I think I probably spun it. I thought he was judging me.

Therapist: It sounds like you're picking up on a theme in your thinking. Do you think it would help to try what's worked at home?

Client: Maybe. Just take it for what it is? [Pause] I'm not sure how to do that exactly with him.

Therapist: You want to practice some here, now?

Client: All right.

## Critique of the Interpersonal and Social Rhythm Therapy Demonstration Vignette

**The following points were made in the critique:**

a. Therapist is using the Social Rhythm Metric form to assist the client in monitoring his daily activities, mood, and interpersonal interactions.
b. The goal of the therapist is to move the client's social rhythm to more stability and less conflict.
c. Therapist uses reflective techniques to allow the client to come to his own assessment of his "spinning" the communication of others.
d. The theme of reading into others' communication is found both at home and at work. Then therapist allows the client to come to this awareness.

**Additional points that could be made:**

a. Therapist alludes to problem-solving techniques that can be used to overcome future issues.
b. Therapist does a great job of drawing the client into assessing his own communication dysfunction rather than pointing it out to him.
c. An objective of this intervention is to enhance the patient's interpersonal skills to reduce an interpersonal conflict that may make him vulnerable to relapse.

**Comments you would like to make:**

_____
_____
_____
_____

**Homework:** An intervention for IPT found in Table 5.5 cites the homework "Identify and Schedule Pleasant Activities" to help the client find a balance to his/her activity level. The exercise "Sleep Pattern Record" teaches sleep induction methods as well as allowing the client to record his/her sleep pattern for the week. Cognitive-behavioral techniques are used to assist in resolving interpersonal disputes. Problem-solving skills may be applied first through didactic, then role-play, and then assigned to be applied to actual life relationships. The exercise "Applying Problem-Solving to Interpersonal Conflict" (*Adult Psychotherapy Homework Planner*, 2nd ed., by Jongsma) is consistent with this IPT approach and may be useful to the therapeutic process. The exercise "Planning for Stability" is designed to help the client think through the issues related to establishing a consistent and healthy routine, including daily schedule, medication management, diet, sleep hygiene, pleasurable activities, and so on (*Addiction Treatment Homework Planner*, 4th ed., by Finley and Lenz). (See www.wiley.com/go/bpdwb)

## Interpersonal and Social Rhythm Therapy Review

1. What are the major emphases of IPSRT?

---

- A thorough assessment of the disorder as well as important past and present interpersonal relationships
- Stabilizing social rhythms
- Addressing interpersonal problems through the use of interpersonal therapy

---

### Talking Points

Regulating the sleep/wake cycle is part of stabilizing social rhythm and an increasingly important factor in mood episode relapse prevention. Having good sleep hygiene is important to establishing and maintaining a good sleep cycle. Consider facilitating a discussion around what good sleep hygiene entails. The following are some key features of good sleep hygiene practices:

- Fix an awakening time and, preferably, a sleep time as well.
- Avoid napping during the day.
- Avoid intake of alcohol, caffeine, and spicy or sugary foods 4 to 6 hours before bedtime.
- Exercise regularly, but not within approximately 2 hours before bed.
- Use comfortable bedding.
- Set a comfortable room temperature. A cool (not cold) bedroom is often the most conducive to sleep.
- Eliminate distracting noise and as much light as possible.
- Reserve the bed for sleep and sex.
- Consider having a light snack before bedtime.
- Practice relaxation techniques before bedtime.
- Occupy your mind with relaxing thoughts or images. Consider assigning a "worry period" or planning period during the late afternoon to address worries.
- Establish a presleep ritual (e.g., a warm bath, a few minutes of reading).
- Get into your favorite sleeping position.
- If you don't fall asleep within 15 to 30 minutes, get up, go into another room, and read until you feel sleepy.

## Interpersonal and Social Rhythm Therapy Review Test Question

1. True or False: The concept of social rhythms refers to the quality of the patient's social relationships, whether they are good (i.e., in rhythm) or poor (i.e., out of rhythm).

    Answer: False

## Chapter References

Bevilacqua, Louis, and Frank M. Dattilio. (2010). *Family Therapy Homework Planner* (2nd ed.). Hoboken, NJ: John Wiley & Sons.

Finley, James R., & Brenda S. Lenz. (2003). *Addiction Treatment Homework Planner* (4th ed.). Hoboken, NJ: John Wiley.

Jongsma, Arthur E. (2006). *Adult Psychotherapy Homework Planner* (2nd ed.). Hoboken, NJ: Wiley.

# Closing Remarks and Resources

As we note on the DVD, it is important to be aware that the research support for any particular EST supports the identified treatment as it was delivered in the studies supporting it. The use of only selected objectives or interventions from ESTs may not be empirically supported.

If you want to incorporate an EST into your treatment plan, it should reflect the major objectives and interventions of the approach. Note that in addition to their primary objectives and interventions, many ESTs have options within them that may or may not be used depending on the client's need (e.g., skills training). Most treatment manuals, books, and other training programs identify the primary objectives and interventions used in the EST.

An existing resource for integrating research-supported treatments into treatment planning is the Practice*Planners*® series[1] of treatment planners. The series contains several books that have integrated goals, objectives, and interventions consistent with those of identified ESTs into treatment plans for several applicable problems and disorders:

- *The Severe and Persistent Mental Illness Treatment Planner* (Berghuis, Jongsma, & Bruce)
- *The Family Therapy Treatment Planner* (Dattilio, Jongsma, & Davis)
- *The Complete Adult Psychotherapy Treatment Planner* (Jongsma, Peterson, & Bruce)
- *The Adolescent Psychotherapy Treatment Planner* (Jongsma, Peterson, McInnis, & Bruce)
- *The Child Psychotherapy Treatment Planner* (Jongsma, Peterson, McInnis, &Bruce)

---

[1]These books are updated frequently; check with the publisher for the latest editions and for further information about the PracticePlanners®.

## Closing Remarks and Resources 51

- *The Veterans and Active Duty Military Psychotherapy Treatment Planner* (Moore & Jongsma)
- *The Addiction Treatment Planner* (Perkinson, Jongsma, & Bruce)
- *The Couples Psychotherapy Treatment Planner* (O'Leary, Heyman, & Jongsma)
- *The Older Adult Psychotherapy Treatment Planner* (Frazer, Hinrichsen, & Jongsma)
- *The School Counseling and School Social Work Treatment Planner* (Knapp, Jongsma, & Dimmitt)
- *The Crisis Counseling and Traumatic Events Treatment Planner* (Kolski, Jongsma, & Myer)

Finally, it is important to remember that the purpose of this series is to demonstrate the process of evidence-based psychotherapy treatment planning for common mental health problems. It is designed to be informational in nature, and does not intend to be a substitute for clinical training in the interventions discussed and demonstrated. In accordance with ethical guidelines, therapists should have competency in the services they deliver.

# APPENDIX A

# A Sample Evidence-Based Treatment Plan for Bipolar Disorder

**Primary Problem:** Bipolar I Disorder, Depressed

**Behavioral Definitions:**

1. Has shown evidence of five (or more) major depressive episode symptoms (i.e., sadness, interest deficiency, guilt, energy loss, concentration deficits, appetite disturbance, psychomotor slowness, sleep disturbance, suicidal thoughts).
2. Exhibits an abnormally and persistently elevated, expansive, or irritable mood with at least three manic symptoms (i.e., inflated self-esteem or grandiosity, decreased need for sleep, pressured speech, flight of ideas, distractibility, increased goal-directed activity or psychomotor agitation, excessive involvement in pleasurable, high-risk behavior).
3. The elevated mood or irritability (mania) causes marked impairment in occupational functioning, social activities, or relationships with others.

**Diagnosis:** Bipolar I Disorder, Depressed, Moderate (296.52)

**Long-Term Goals:**

1. Normalize energy level and return to usual activities, good judgment, stable mood, more realistic expectations, and goal-directed behavior.
2. Develop healthy cognitive patterns and beliefs about self and the world that lead to alleviation and help prevent the relapse of manic-depression symptoms.
3. Alleviate depressed mood and return to previous level of effective functioning.

| Objectives | Interventions |
|---|---|
| 1. Describe mood state, energy level, amount of control over thoughts, and sleeping pattern. | 1. Assess the client for classic signs of elevated, expansive, or irritable mood: pressured speech, high-risk behavior, euphoria, flight of ideas, reduced need for sleep, inflated self-esteem, high energy, etc.<br>2. Assess the client's level of elation: hypomanic, manic, or psychotic and the degree of impact on the client's social, occupational, and interpersonal functioning.<br>3. Assess the client for signs of depression and whether there is evidence of cycling from depression to mania or hypomania. |

# Appendix A

| Objectives | Interventions |
|---|---|
| 2. Complete psychological testing to assess communication patterns within the family or with significant others. | 1. Arrange for the administration of an objective assessment instrument for evaluating communication patterns with family/significant others, particularly expressed emotion (e.g., Perceived Criticism Scale by Hooley and Teasdale); evaluate results and process feedback with the client and family. |
| 3. Cooperate with a psychiatric evaluation as to the need for medication and/or hospitalization to stabilize mood and energy. | 1. Arrange for a psychiatric evaluation of the client for pharmacotherapy (e.g., Lithium carbonate, Depakote, Lamictil). |
| | 2. Monitor the client's reaction to the psychotropic medication (e.g., compliance, side effects, and effectiveness) and report reactions to prescribing physician. |
| | 3. Monitor the client's symptom improvement toward stabilization sufficient to allow participation in psychotherapy. |
| 4. Verbalize an understanding of the causes for, symptoms of, and treatment of manic, hypomanic, mixed, and/or depressive episode. | 1. Teach the client, family, and relevant others, using all modalities necessary, about the signs, symptoms, and phasic relapsing nature of the client's mood episodes; destigmatize and normalize. |
| | 2. Teach the client a stress diathesis model of bipolar disorder that emphasizes the strong role of a biological predisposition to mood episodes that is vulnerable to stresses that are manageable and the need for medication compliance (or assign "Why I Dislike Taking My Medication" in the *Adult Psychotherapy Homework Planner*, 2nd ed., by Jongsma). |
| | 3. Provide the client with a rationale for treatment involving ongoing medication and psychosocial treatment to recognize, manage, and reduce biological and psychological vulnerabilities that could precipitate relapse. |
| 5. Attend group psychoeducational sessions designed to inform members as to the nature of and causes for bipolar disorder, as well as emphasize the need to comply with medication and other treatment and ways to minimize relapse. | 1. Conduct a series of 21 group sessions that teach clients the psychological, biological, and social influences in development of BPD, its biological and psychological treatment, illness management skills (e.g., early warning signs, common triggers, coping strategies), problem solving focused on life goals, and a personal care plan that emphasizes a regular sleep routine and stress regulation. |

*(continued)*

| Objectives | Interventions |
|---|---|
| 6. Family members learn about bipolar disorder, factors that influence it, the role of medication and therapy, while learning skills that help manage it and improve the quality of life of the family and its members. | 1. Conduct psychoeducation with family members emphasizing the biological nature of bipolar disorder, the need for medication and medication adherence, risk factors for relapse such as personal and interpersonal triggers, and the importance of communication, problem solving, and early episode intervention.<br>2. Using structured exercises, teach the family that strong negative expressed emotion (e.g., hostility, pity, criticism) can trigger relapse of bipolar episodes; use role-play, modeling, and feedback to teach respectful, reflective, attentive, active listening and problem-solving skills (see *Bipolar Disorder: A Family-Focused Approach* by Miklowitz and Goldstein).<br>3. Assign the client and family homework exercises to use and record use of newly learned communication enhancement therapy skills; process results in session. |

# APPENDIX B

# Chapter Review Test Questions and Answers Explained

## Chapter 1: What Is Bipolar Disorder?

1. A 22-year-old male presents to his family physician with pervasive sadness, loss of appetite, and sleeplessness for three weeks. He complains of feeling tired and has difficulty concentrating on his schoolwork. He has dropped out of activities with friends that he previously enjoyed. His physician has ruled out medical and substance etiologies and is considering the diagnosis of Major Depressive Disorder (MDD). To determine if this is the correct mood disorder diagnosis, which of the following does the physician need to do?

    A. Assess for an abuse history
    B. Assess for past mood episodes
    C. Assess the past treatment history
    D. Explore the family history of mood disorders

    A. *Incorrect*: Although this might be important to assess, it will not help specify which mood disorder diagnosis is best supported.
    B. *Correct*: In diagnosing mood disorders, it is necessary to assess present and *past* mood episodes. For example, if there is a history of a past hypomanic episode, the patient's diagnosis would be Bipolar II Disorder; whereas, if there are no past hypomanic, manic, or mixed episodes, MDD would be the supported mood disorder diagnosis.
    C. *Incorrect*: Although this might be important to assess, it does not provide direct evidence of past mood episodes, which is what the physician needs to assess to determine the correct mood disorder diagnosis. For example, past treatment could be based on misdiagnosis or reflect an inappropriate treatment choice.
    D. *Incorrect*: Although this might be important to assess, it does not help specify which mood disorder diagnosis is best supported.

2. True or False: A person with a diagnosis of a mood disorder may find that the diagnosis could accurately change over time (e.g., be one diagnosis a year ago and another currently).

True. Mood disorder diagnoses may accurately change over time depending on subsequent mood episodes. For example, a person whose first mood episode is depressive will have a mood disorder diagnosis of Major Depressive Disorder at that time. If he or she subsequently experiences a manic or hypomanic episode, the diagnosis would be changed at that time to reflect a bipolar disorder.

## Chapter 2: What Are the Six Steps in Building a Treatment Plan?

1. As noted previously, some patients with bipolar disorder may show grandiose delusions, while others may not. Some may be engaging in several high-risk behaviors, while others may not. In which step of treatment planning would you record the particular expressions of bipolar disorder for your individual client?

   A. Creating short-term objectives
   B. Describing the problem's manifestations
   C. Identifying the primary problem
   D. Selecting treatment interventions

   A. *Incorrect*: Expressions of the disorder—also referred to as manifestations, features, or symptoms—are described in Step 2 of treatment planning. They are not objectives for the client to achieve.
   B. *Correct*: Expressions of the disorder—also referred to as manifestations, features, or symptoms—are described in Step 2 of treatment planning.
   C. *Incorrect*: Expressions of the disorder—also referred to as manifestations, features, or symptoms—are described in Step 2 of treatment planning. They are expressions of the primary problem: the bipolar disorder.
   D. *Incorrect*: Expressions of the disorder—also referred to as manifestations, features, or symptoms—are described in Step 2 of treatment planning. They are not interventions that the therapist will use to help the client achieve his or her objectives.

2. The statement "Learn and implement problem-solving skills to manage problems and reduce the risk of mood episodes" is an example of a statement describing which of the following elements of a psychotherapy treatment plan?

   A. A primary problem
   B. A short-term objective

C. A symptom manifestation
   D. A treatment intervention
      A. *Incorrect*: The primary problem (Step 1 in treatment planning) is the summary description, usually in diagnostic terms, of the client's primary problem.
      B. *Correct*: This is a short-term objective (Step 5 in treatment planning). It describes a desired action of the client that is likely to help him or her reach a treatment goal.
      C. *Incorrect*: Symptom manifestations (Step 2 in treatment planning) describe the client's particular expression (i.e., features or symptoms) of the primary problem.
      D. *Incorrect*: A treatment intervention (Step 6 in treatment planning) describes the therapist's actions designed to help the client achieve his or her short-term objectives.

# Chapter 3: What Is the Brief History of the Empirically Supported Treatments Movement?

1. Which statement best describes the process used to identify ESTs?
   A. Consumers of mental health services nominated therapies.
   B. Experts came to a consensus based on their experiences with the treatments.
   C. Researchers submitted their works.
   D. Task groups reviewed the literature using clearly defined selection criteria for ESTs.
      A. *Incorrect*: Mental health professionals selected ESTs.
      B. *Incorrect*: Expert consensus was not the method used to identify ESTs.
      C. *Incorrect*: Empirical works in the existing literature were reviewed to identify ESTs.
      D. *Correct*: Review groups consisting of mental health professionals selected ESTs based on predetermined criteria such as *well-established* and *probably efficacious*.

2. Based on the differences in their criteria, in which of the following ways are *well-established* treatments different from those classified as *probably efficacious*?
   A. Only *probably efficacious* allowed the use of a single-case design experiment.
   B. Only *well-established* allowed studies comparing the treatment to a psychological placebo.
   C. Only *well-established* required demonstration by at least two different, independent investigators or investigating teams.
   D. Only *well-established* allowed studies comparing the treatment to a pill placebo.

A. *Incorrect*: Both sets of criteria allowed use of single-subject designs. *Well-established* required a larger series than did *probably efficacious* (see II under Well-Established and III under Probably Efficacious).
B. *Incorrect*: Studies using comparison to psychological placebos were acceptable in both sets of criteria (see IA under Well-Established and II under Probably Efficacious).
C. *Correct*: One of the primary differences between treatments classified as *well-established* and those classified as *probably efficacious* is that *well-established* therapies have had their efficacy demonstrated by at least two different, independent investigators (see V under Well-Established).
D. *Incorrect*: Studies using comparison to pill placebos were acceptable in both sets of criteria (see IA under Well-Established and II under Probably Efficacious).

## Chapter 4: What Are the Identified Empirically Supported Treatments for Bipolar Disorder?

1. According to APA's Division 12, The Society of Clinical Psychology, which of the following has met their criteria for a well-established psychological treatment for bipolar depression?
   A. Cognitive-behavioral therapy (CBT)
   B. Interpersonal and social rhythm therapy (IPSRT)
   C. Family-focused therapy (FFT)
   D. Group psychoeducation (GP)
      A. *Incorrect*: The efficacy of CBT has not met this level of evidence as defined by this organization. Rather, it is currently classified as probably efficacious.
      B. *Incorrect*: The efficacy of IPSRT has not met this level of evidence as defined by this organization. Like CBT, it is currently classified as probably efficacious.
      C. *Correct*: FFT has met this organization's highest level of evidence for the treatment of bipolar depression.
      D. *Incorrect*: Group psychoeducation has met this organization's highest level of evidence for the treatment of bipolar mania, but not bipolar depression.

2. Which of the following best describes the outcome of the Systematic Treatment Enhancement Program for Bipolar Disorder (STEP-BD) study, in which cognitive-behavioral therapy (CBT), interpersonal and social rhythm therapy

(IPSRT), and family-focused therapy (FBT) were compared to a control psychological treatment while all participants were also on medication?

A. CBT was associated with a faster recovery rate from acute depression than all other treatments.
B. CBT, FFT, and IPSRT were all associated with a faster recovery rate from acute depression than the control treatment.
C. FFT was associated with a faster recovery rate from acute depression than all other treatments.
D. IPSRT was associated with a faster recovery rate from acute depression than all other treatments.
   A. *Incorrect*: In the STEP-BD, being in any of the three evidence-based psychotherapies, including CBT, was associated with a faster recovery rate from acute depression than being in collaborative care.
   B. *Correct*: In the STEP-BD, being in any of the three evidence-based psychotherapies was associated with a faster recovery rate from acute depression than being in collaborative care.
   C. *Incorrect*: In the STEP-BD, being in any of the three evidence-based psychotherapies, including FFT, was associated with a faster recovery rate from acute depression than being in collaborative care.
   D. *Incorrect*: In the STEP-BD, being in any of the three evidence-based psychotherapies, including IPSRT, was associated with a faster recovery rate from acute depression than being in collaborative care.

## Chapter 5: How Do You Integrate ESTs Into Treatment Planning?
### Psychoeducation

1. Although psychoeducation permeates most research-supported treatments for bipolar disorder, which of the following forms of it is a well-established psychological treatment for bipolar mania, according to Division 12 of the APA?

   A. Cognitive-behavioral therapy (CBT)
   B. Family-focused therapy (FFT)
   C. Group psychoeducation (GP)
   D. Individual psychoeducation (IP)
      A. *Incorrect*: Although CBT has a psychoeducation emphasis as part of the overall treatment approach, CBT is not a form of psychoeducation that is well-established psychological treatment for bipolar mania.
      B. *Incorrect*: Although FFT has a psychoeducation emphasis as part of the overall treatment approach, FFT is not a form of psychoeducation that

is well-established psychological treatment for bipolar mania. The treatment is a well-established intervention for bipolar depression, however.
   C. *Correct*: Group psychoeducation (e.g., *The Life Goals Program* by Bauer and McBride [2003]) is a well-established psychological treatment for bipolar mania, according to Division 12 of the APA.
   D. *Incorrect*: Although individual psychoeducation has demonstrated efficacy in the treatment of bipolar mania, the level of evidence supporting it has not met the criteria of a well-established psychological treatment used by Division 12 of the APA.

## Cognitive-Behavioral Therapy

1. True or False: Cognitive therapy grew out of its use with unipolar depression. In its application to mania, it also targets the overly positive and grandiose thoughts characteristic of manic episodes.

   True.     Cognitive therapies (or CBT) for bipolar disorder involves its conventional emphases, such as learning the connection between thinking, emotion, and mood; identifying and challenging maladaptive thoughts and beliefs. In its application to mania, there is also an emphasis on thoughts as symptoms of mania and teaching clients ways to recognize and address them.

## Family-Focused Therapy

1. Which of the following are the core interventions of family-focused therapy (FFT)?
   a. Psychoeducation about the biological basis of bipolar disorder and the need for medication adherence.
   b. Communication skills training that minimizes negative expressed emotion.
   c. Problem-solving skills training to reduce the risk that problems may lead to a relapse of mood episodes.
   d. Psychoeducation, communication enhancement training, and problem-solving skills training.
      A. *Incorrect*: This is one theme of one of the three core interventions used in FFT: psychoeducation.
      B. *Incorrect*: This is one of three core interventions of FFT: communication enhancement training.
      C. *Incorrect*: This is one of three core interventions of FFT: problem-solving skills training.
      D. *Correct*: Psychoeducation, communication enhancement training, and problem-solving skills training are the core interventions of FFT, within

which several objectives are targeted (e.g., learning about the biological basis of bipolar disorder, developing a relapse management plan, improving interpersonal relationships among family members).

## Interpersonal and Social Rhythm Therapy

1. True or False: The concept of social rhythms refers to the quality of the patient's social relationships, whether they are good (i.e., in rhythm) or poor (i.e., out of rhythm).

   False: The concept of social rhythm refers to the nature of the patient's daily activity, including the types of activities, the level of activity, their regularity, and balance. It includes considerations such as when patients arise, go to sleep, eat, socialize, and exercise. Patients are taught how to track and regulate their daily routines, including their sleep/wake cycles, in an effort to balance stimulation and ensure rest.

# STUDY PACKAGE
# CONTINUING EDUCATION
# CREDIT INFORMATION

## Evidence-Based Treatment Planning for Bipolar Disorder

Our goal is to provide you with current, accurate and practical information from the most experienced and knowledgeable speakers and authors.

Listed below are the continuing education credit(s) currently available for this self-study package. *Please note: Your state licensing board dictates whether self study is an acceptable form of continuing education. Please refer to your state rules and regulations.*

**Counselors**: CMI Education Institute, Inc. is an approved provider of the National Board of Certified Counselors, NBCC Provider #: 5637. We adhere to NBCC Continuing Education Guidelines. This self-study package qualifies for **3.25** contact hours.

**Social Workers**: CMI Education Institute, Inc., #1062, is approved as a provider for social work continuing education by the Association of Social Work Boards (ASWB), 400 South Ridge Parkway, Suite B, Culpeper VA 22701. www.aswb.org. CMI Education Institute, Inc. maintains responsibility for the program. Licensed Social Workers should contact their regulatory board to determine course approval. Social Workers will receive **3.25** (clinical) continuing education clock hours for completing this self-study package. Course Level: All Levels.

**Marriage and Family Therapists**: This activity consists of **3.25** hours of continuing education instruction. Credit requirements and approvals vary per state board regulations. Please save the course outline, the certificate of completion you receive from this self-study activity and contact your state board or organization to determine specific filing requirements.

**Psychologists**: CMI Education Institute, Inc. is approved by the American Psychological Association to sponsor continuing education for psychologists. CMI maintains responsibility for this program and its content. CMI is offering these self-study materials for **3.0** hours of continuing education credit.

**Addiction Counselors**: CMI Education Institute, Inc. is an approved provider of continuing education by the National Association of Alcoholism & Drug Abuse Counselors (NAADAC), provider #: 00131. This self-study package qualifies for **4.0** contact hours.

**Nurses/Nurse Practitioners/Clinical Nurse Specialists:** This activity meets the criteria for an American Nurses Credentialing Center (ANCC) Activity CMI Education Institute, Inc. is an approved sponsor by the American Psychological Association, which is recognized by the ANCC for behavioral health related activities.

This self-study activity qualifies for **3.0** contact hours.

**Other Professions**: This activity qualifies for **3.25** clock hours of instructional content as required by many national, state and local licensing boards and professional organizations. Retain your certificate of completion and contact your board or organization for specific filing requirements.

---

For additional forms and information on other Premier Education Solutions products, contact: **Customer Service; CMI Education;** P.O. Box 1000; Eau Claire, WI 54702 (Toll Free, 7 a.m.-5 p.m. central time, 800-844-8260). www.cmieducation.org

## Procedures:

1. Review the materials (publication and DVD).

2. If seeking credit, complete the posttest/evaluation form:

    -Complete posttest/evaluation in entirety; including your email address for the most prompt receipt of your certificate of completion.

    -Upon completion, mail to the address listed on the form along with the CE fee stated on the test. Tests will not be processed without the CE fee included.

    -Completed posttests must be received 6 months from the date of purchase.

Your completed posttest/evaluation will be graded. If you receive a passing score (70% and above), you will be emailed/faxed/mailed a certificate of successful completion with earned continuing education credits. (Please include your email address on the posttest/evaluation form for fastest response) If you do not pass the posttest, you will be sent a letter via email indicating areas of deficiency, and another posttest to complete. The posttest must be resubmitted and receive a passing grade before credit can be awarded. We will allow you to re-take as many times as necessary (with no additional fee) to receive a passing grade.

If you have any questions, please feel free to contact our customer service department at 1.800.844.8260.

# CMI Education Institute

A Non-Profit Organization Connecting Knowledge with Need Since 1979

For additional forms and information on other Premier Education Solutions products, contact: **Customer Service; CMI Education;**
P.O. Box 1000; Eau Claire, WI 54702 (Toll Free, 7 a.m.-5 p.m. central time, 800-844-8260). www.cmieducation.org

# Evidence-Based Treatment Planning for Bipolar Disorder
Post Test/Evaluation Form

ZNT044635

P.O. Box 1000
Eau Claire, WI 54702
(800) 844-8260

Any persons interested in receiving credit may photocopy this form, complete and return with a payment of $15.00 per person CE fee. A certificate of successful completion will be sent to you. To receive your certificate sooner than two weeks, rush processing is available for a fee of $10. Please attach check or include credit card information below.

| For office use only |
|---|
| Rcvd. _____ |
| Graded _____ |
| Cert. mld. _____ |

**Mail to: CMI Education, PO Box 1000, Eau Claire, WI 54702 or fax to: CMI Education (800) 554-9775 (fax both sides of page)**

C.E. Fee: $15.00: (Rush Process Fee: $10) Total to be charged: _____
Credit card #_____ Exp. Date:_____
Signature: _____
V-Code*_____ (*MC/VISA/Discover: last 3-digit # on signature panel on back of card.) (*American Express: 4-digit # above account # on face of card.)

Name (please print): _____  _____  _____
                              LAST                                FIRST                                M.I.
Address: _____ Daytime Phone: _____
City: _____ State: _____ Zip: _____
Signature: _____ Email: _____ Fax: _____
• Date you completed the CMI Independent Package: _____
• Actual time (# of hours) taken to complete this offering: _____ hours

## GENERAL COMMENTS
Please circle the number indicating your rating of each of the following items.

|  | Excellent |  |  |  | Poor |
|---|---|---|---|---|---|
| Relevance of objectives to overall goal | 5 | 4 | 3 | 2 | 1 |
| Effectiveness of the teaching/learning methods | 5 | 4 | 3 | 2 | 1 |
| Achievement of your personal objectives for completing this course | 5 | 4 | 3 | 2 | 1 |
| Similarity of program content to its description | 5 | 4 | 3 | 2 | 1 |
| Overall rating of package | 5 | 4 | 3 | 2 | 1 |
| How much did you learn as a result of this program? (5 being a great deal - 1 being very little) | 5 | 4 | 3 | 2 | 1 |

## PROGRAM OBJECTIVES
At the completion of this package, I have been able to achieve these seminar objectives:

| | | |
|---|---|---|
| Explain the process used to diagnose mood disorders including bipolar disorders | Yes | No |
| List the six steps in building a clear psychotherapy treatment plan | Yes | No |
| Examine how empirically supported treatments for bipolar disorder have been identified | Yes | No |
| Illustrate objectives and treatment interventions consistent with those of identified empirically supported treatments for bipolar disorder | Yes | No |
| Explain how to construct a psychotherapy treatment plan and inform it with objectives and treatment interventions consistent with those identified empirically supported treatments for bipolar disorder | Yes | No |
| | Yes | No |

## PARTICIPANT PROFILE
1. Job Title _____ Employment Setting _____
2. Who paid the cost for this set? Self _____ Employer _____
3. Do you utilize the internet? Yes _____ No _____ If so, where? Home _____ Work _____
4. What information did you hope to get from this audio/video/manual set? _____

ZNT044635                                          CE Release Date: 2/09/2012

**Post Seminar Test Questions**

1. According to psychiatric diagnostic classification systems, which of the following mood episodes must accompany at least one depressive episode to meet criteria for Bipolar II disorder?
   A. A hypomanic episode
   B. A manic episode
   C. A mixed episode
   D. An additional depressive episode

2. Which of the following changes in sleep is commonly seen during a manic episode?
   A. Decreased total sleep time from normal
   B. Increased nightmares from normal
   C. Increased total sleep time from normal
   D. The development of sleep apnea

3. A therapist decides to include cognitive restructuring as part of the treatment plan for her client with bipolar depression. In which of the following steps in the treatment planning process should this be recorded?
   A. Creating short-term objectives
   B. Describing the problem's manifestations
   C. Selecting therapeutic interventions
   D. Specifying long-term goals

4. A treatment plan contains the sentence, "Learn and implement skills designed to help prevent the relapse of depressive episodes." In which of the following steps in the treatment planning process would this be recorded?
   A. Creating short-term objectives
   B. Describing the problem's manifestations
   C. Selecting therapeutic interventions
   D. Specifying long-term goals

5. According to several reviewers of the psychotherapy outcome literature cited in this program, which of the following interventions is NOT cited as an evidence-based treatment for bipolar depression (as opposed to bipolar mania)?
   A. Cognitive behavioral therapy
   B. Family-focused therapy
   C. Interpersonal and social rhythm therapy
   D. Systematic care

6. According to this program, which of the following research-supported treatments places a strong emphasis on regulating a client's activity level, including sleep and waking patterns?
   A. Group psychoeducation
   B. Family-focused therapy
   C. Interpersonal and social rhythm therapy
   D. Systematic care

7. Which of the following is one of three primary emphases of family-focused therapy?
   A. Communication enhancement training
   B. Exposure therapy
   C. Interpersonal therapy
   D. Progressive muscle relaxation training

8. According to this program, some reviewers of the psychotherapy treatment outcome literature for bipolar disorder (e.g., Miklowitz, 2008) have suggested that one of the means through which adjunctive, evidence-based psychotherapies improve outcomes is by increasing medication compliance.
   A. TRUE
   B. FALSE

9. According to this program, the American Psychological Association defines an evidence-based practice as the integration of the best available research with clinical expertise in the context of patient characteristics, culture, and preferences.
   A. TRUE
   B. FALSE

10. In identifying the evidence-based treatments cited in this program, the authors (i.e., Jongsma & Bruce) have used which of the following methods?
    A. Establishing their own specific criteria for research support and citing those treatments that meet them
    B. Identifying patterns of agreement across reviewers, review groups, and evidence-based practice guideline developers
    C. Identifying treatments most preferred by patients/client
    D. Identifying treatments most preferred by therapists

## Post Seminar Test Questions Continued

11. According to psychiatric diagnostic classification systems, which of the following mood episodes must be evident in the patient's history in order to diagnose Bipolar I disorder?
A. A Hypomanic Episode
B. A Hypomanic or Major Depressive Episode
C. Major Depressive Episode
D. A Manic or Mixed Episode

12. For the last month, Jennifer, a 24-year-old married female, has been extremely tired and sad. She has little interest in activities that she used to enjoy, sleeps excessively, and has gained 8 pounds. She describes herself as useless and lazy. The kind of mood episode from which Jennifer is suffering could be seen in which of the following mood disorders?
A. Bipolar I Disorder
B. Bipolar II Disorder
C. Either A or B
D. Neither A nor B

13. In reference to question 2, Jennifer's expression of depression, including her loss of interest, excessive sleeping, and weight gain would be recorded in which of the following steps in the treatment planning process discussed in this program?
A. Creating short-term objectives
B. Describing the problem's manifestations
C. Selecting therapeutic interventions
D. Specifying long-term goals

14. As discussed in this program, which of the following requirements was unique to APA Division 12's criteria for a well-established treatment, differentiating it from lesser levels of evidence such as probably efficacious?
A. Independent replication of efficacy studies was required.
B. Use of pill placebos in efficacy studies was required.
C. Use of psychological placebos in efficacy studies was required.
D. Use of random assignment in efficacy studies was required.

15. According to several reviewers of the psychotherapy outcome literature cited in this program, which of the following interventions has the highest level of evidence supporting its efficacy in the treatment of bipolar mania (as opposed to bipolar depression)?
A. Cognitive behavioral therapy
B. Group psychoeducation
C. Family-focused therapy
D. Interpersonal and social rhythm therapy

16. According to this program, which of the following research-supported treatments for bipolar depression places a strong emphasis on reducing expressed emotion through the use on communication enhancement and problem-solving skills training?
A. Cognitive behavioral therapy
B. Group psychoeducation
C. Family-focused therapy
D. Interpersonal and social rhythm therapy

17. According to this program, which of the following research-supported treatments for bipolar depression places a strong emphasis on understanding and resolving problems related to important past and/or present relationships in the patient's life?
A. Cognitive behavioral therapy
B. Group psychoeducation
C. Family-focused therapy
D. Interpersonal and social rhythm therapy

18. Which of the following is an intervention common to most research-supported treatments for bipolar disorder discussed in this program?
A. Communication training
B. Exposure therapy
C. Interpersonal therapy
D. Psychoeducation

**Post Seminar Test Questions Continued**

19. As discussed in this program, the Systematic Treatment Enhancement Program for Bipolar Disorder (STEP-BD) investigated the efficacy of three evidence-based psychosocial treatments, family-focused therapy, interpersonal and social rhythm therapy and cognitive behavioral therapy, as well as a control treatment called collaborative care. Results of the study showed no differences in outcome across the four therapies.
A. TRUE
B. FALSE

20. Which of the following best describes the approach to creating an evidence-based treatment plan for bipolar disorder that is recommended in this program?
A. The therapist conducts family-focused therapy.
B. The therapist conducts group psychoeducation.
C. The therapist incorporates into therapy the objectives and interventions consistent with research-supported treatments for bipolar disorder.
D. The therapist incorporates into therapy the use of an objective measure of bipolar disorder to track treatment progress.